Wendell

1947

THOMAS WOLFE

THOMAS WOLFE

Thomas Wolfe

BY HERBERT J. MULLER

THE MAKERS OF MODERN LITERATURE

New Directions Books - Norfolk, Connecticut

MANUFACTURED IN THE UNITED STATES
BY THE VAIL-BALLOU PRESS

*New Directions Books are published by
James Laughlin*

NEW YORK OFFICE—500 FIFTH AVENUE—18

To Herbert LeSourd Creek,

in gratitude, affection, and respect.

CONTENTS

1. ON MYTHS AND LEGENDS

THE LEGEND OF THOMAS WOLFE IS DEPRESSINGLY FAMILIAR. The story goes that he filled ledgers with millions of words and then, with the help of an editor, scissors and paste, finally managed to fashion two long novels out of them, *Look Homeward, Angel* and *Of Time and the River*. They were presumably the life story of a huge, frenzied fellow called Eugene Gant who had an insane passion to walk a million streets, read a million books, make love to a million women—to eat, see, know, feel everything under the sun. They were actually the life story of Wolfe himself, and he recorded his many disagreeable memories so literally that he caused an uproar in his hometown. (It's all right to put us in your book, complained the gentlest of his neighbors, but you might leave out our address and telephone number.) Wolfe was completely surprised, and profoundly distressed; so he started all over again. This time he filled wooden packing cases with the story of another frenzied fellow, called George Webber. Nevertheless he was still writing his autobiography. Then, when only thirty-seven years old, he died. He left more than a million words, from which a new editor fashioned two more long novels, *The Web and the Rock* and *You Can't Go Home Again*. Altogether, it is an absurdly romantic legend; and it is essentially true. At least it is true enough to make Thomas Wolfe look somewhat out of place in the company of the Makers of Modern Literature.

Offhand, indeed, there would seem to be little excuse for a critical study of Wolfe. His elemental powers are remarkable but they are also obvious; so are his elementary faults. He offers critics plenty of opportunity to exercise their eloquence in celebrating his powers, or their wit in ridiculing his faults; he offers little opportunity for acute analysis, subtle appreciation, or the knowing kind of criticism that distinguishes this age. Nor is the reader's judgment of his work likely to be affected much by criticism. Whether one is impressed most by his splendid gifts or by his shocking sins as an artist is chiefly a matter of temperament. One may have to learn to like caviar; one does not cultivate a taste for roast beef. Moreover, Wolfe was not a pioneer, a leader, or an "influence" of the kind beloved by literary historians. He experimented with some technical devices picked up from Joyce and others, he disregarded much more that novelists have learned about their craft, he finally went his own way; but it was not a new way. He made no original contribution to the methods and materials of fiction, has had no notable effect on contemporary literature that I am aware of. For the best in him remains elemental and is literally inimitable. Only his faults can be imitated readily, and they are the kind that young writers come by naturally, all by themselves.

Yet Wolfe stands out, and not merely as a romantic or freakish figure. Although he has been patronized as a gifted amateur or magnificent adolescent, he has also been flattered, more than any other contemporary American novelist, by comparisons to the great novelists of the past, such as Balzac, Dickens, Melville and Dostoyevsky. He would remain important for the simple reason that he created many unforgettable characters and scenes, a whole swarming world; for if this primal creative power ultimately defies analysis, it is nevertheless what distinguishes major from minor fiction. Wolfe is also important, however, because he grappled with the fundamental issues of modern life and literature. His work is not only a symptom of this age, reflecting its deep confusions and discords, but finally a significant criticism of it. If most of our leading writers have been intellectually more acute than he, more resourceful in their experimentation with new methods and materials, more brilliant in their technical achievements, none have been more honest and thorough-going in their effort to come to terms with their world. In his simplicity Wolfe forces us back to elementary principles, the first and last things that subtle, sophisticated writers are apt to overlook. And at that his simplicity is deceptive. It is atop complexity as well as beneath it; Wolfe was fully aware of the complexities of modern life, if only because of his mad hunger to experience everything; and so he always went through them, not around them. Unlike most of his intellectual betters, he was never taken in by the fashionable simplicities of

3

his time—the cults of the wastelanders, the esthetes, the literary communists, the literary agrarians, the literary primitives.

Hence we might pause to get our bearings. The most illuminating perspective on Wolfe's life and work can be got, I believe, by a roundabout approach through a term that has recently become popular in literary circles—the term *myth*. We have rediscovered that a myth is not simply a pretty fancy, a charming memento of the childhood of the race, or something to be "exploded." The great myths—as of Prometheus, of Jacob and his sons, of the resurrection of Christ—symbolize the fundamental meanings of human existence, the timeless patterns or cycles of life and death, the timeless problems of love and justice. They represent, in the words of Mark Schorer, "a large, controlling image . . . which gives philosophical meaning to the facts of ordinary life, that is to say, which has organizing value for experience." In other words, the myth is not a way of disguising or evading the shocking facts of life but a way of ordering and accepting them. It is an indispensable way, since the facts do not really speak for themselves.

All imaginative literature may be conceived as sophisticated mythology, or philosophy as rationalized mythology, or religious dogma as fossilized mythology. In the beginning was the word as *mythos*, the ancient, concrete story of the origin and nature of the world; from this developed the *epos*, or symbolical narrative, and finally the *logos*, the word as rational explanation. The three stages correspond to the development of language, from literal concreteness through metaphor to abstraction, and finally correspond to the history of thought and knowledge.[1] Today, literature, philosophy, religion, and even science are still mythologies in that they are alike founded on some imaginative scheme, and ultimately speak in metaphor. None gives us the whole truth and nothing but the truth; all are selections from experience, versions of the supreme metaphor Reality. If we believe that some one version contains the essential truth, then all the others are still more plainly mythologies; but in any event all serve the same purpose of organizing experience. Likewise society itself is founded on myths, and could not exist without them. They survive not only as old superstitions but as tradition; they are the common meanings, faiths, purposes that hold a group together and constitute its "way of life."

In literature, more particularly, we may trace the development from myth to heroic legend, to romance, to realistic story. Yet all great literature still tends to resemble or become myth. This is most apparent in consciously allegorical or symbolical work, such as *The Divine Comedy*, *The Faery Queen, Paradise Lost, Prometheus Unbound* and *Faust*. It is no less true of *Hamlet* and *The Misanthrope*, of *War and Peace, Vanity Fair, The Brothers Karamazov* and *The Return of the Native*. As Thomas Mann remarks, the mythical is the typical; it is the pri-

[1] Plato is the clearest example of this development, even apart from the myths he introduced into his dialogues. Although it is conventional to distinguish his poetry from his philosophy, his philosophy is as plainly a development from myth. His Ideas are not purely logical concepts but images, divine symbols; he is personifying the world of reason as the early myths personified the world of nature. And no less mythical, in this sense, are such concepts as Schopenhauer's Will.

5

meval norm of life, "the pious formula into which life flows when it reproduces its traits out of the unconscious." At the same time, we may distinguish the conscious use of mythical material, the deliberate recreation of the myth. In modern literature, the supreme example is Mann's Joseph story.

Such purposes are also conscious in Thomas Wolfe, however; and here is the lead to the main import of his work. From the outset he felt that he "belonged with the Mythmakers," and conceived his task in terms of the myth. "O lost!" runs the refrain of *Look Homeward, Angel*, a "Story of the Buried Life." "Remembering speechlessly we seek the great forgotten language, the lost lane-end into heaven, a stone, a leaf, an unfound door." The central theme of Wolfe's entire work was the search for a father and a home, for "the image of a strength and wisdom external to his need and superior to his hunger, to which the belief and power of his own life could be united." His specific theme, in other words, is the central problem of all writers today, in a "realistic" age that prides itself upon facing the facts but is swamped by them. Our vast store of knowledge is too often a jumble of undigested or indigestible facts, our experience too often a violent succession of facts without philosophical meaning or immediately with all too shocking meaning. We still live by myths, for the most part unconsciously; we too seldom have a clear, steady image, a coherent mythology. And the key to Wolfe's achievement is the gradual widening and deepening of the implications of his theme, the transformation of a private legend into a public myth—a modern *Pilgrim's Progress.*

6

ON MYTHS AND LEGENDS

In his quest Wolfe was as terribly confused as terribly sincere; no other important modern writer has appeared so often naïve, extravagant, maudlin, ludicrous. He began like most young writers, only more so: writing the story of his own life in capital letters, underlining and italicizing it, adding exclamation points. Specifically, the main trouble was that his myth was the religion of genius, his controlling image the romantic image of the God-like artist as one possessed, set apart from his fellowmen, privileged to demand of them not merely a living but an immortal life. Tumult is the insignia of this artist, the proof of his depth and sincerity; he seethes with imperishable thoughts, and then seethes still more because his fellows seem willing to let these thoughts perish. For Wolfe this image was further intensified and distorted by typically American experience. He was a young writer in the small town, whose relatives and neighbors regarded him as queer; he was a country boy dazzled by the big city, and then lost in it; he was a yokel at once awed and infuriated by the wealthy, the cultured, the sophisticated; he was a proud Southerner who had rebelled against his own people, yet was resentful and suspicious of the Yankee; he was a proud American who knew that Europe was effete, but had to go there to find real culture. He was also a child of the reckless 'twenties, homeless among all the boys who were making good, bitterly aware that they were not making for good, yet infected by the gross popular myths he despised. For his image of the privileged artist, above all ordinary social obligations, was a variant of the popular image of the rugged individual, another symbol of an age of special privilege without social responsibility.

7

Nevertheless Wolfe kept his head better than most of his contemporaries. Despite his intense concern with himself and with the Artist he had created in his own image, he was always close to the oldest, deepest simplicities: the good earth, the life of common men, the common destiny of mortality, the flow of time and the river. In particular, he was close to native traditions, which in the 'twenties and 'thirties were suspect among intellectuals on both the Right and the Left. Like many other writers, he often felt profoundly alienated from America, but he was still more profoundly drawn to it; the very violence of his revulsions indicated the strength of its hold on him; and all his flights to Europe, or into angry rhetoric, were transient and unavailing. From the beginning, the greatness of America had been one of his main themes, if only because he needed a great subject to prove the greatness he so passionately and naively aspired to. In time he came, with increasing clarity and sobriety, to identify the legend of his hunger as an American legend, and to seek his image in the history and the destiny of the nation.

What brought Wolfe to his social senses was the great depression that ended the 'twenties. In his constant prowlings about New York he saw everywhere the human wreckage of the social collapse, the appalling incongruity of the few rotten in their wealth and the many helpless in their wretched poverty. He came to define the root evil as "single selfishness and compulsive greed." He recognized it as an ancient evil but also as the special vice of American life, in its strident individualism and blatant materialism. At the same time, however, Wolfe was deeply impressed by the fortitude of the people. He came to feel a solidarity with them in their suffering and their ability to survive. He came to realize that he was not actually singular, that his prized individuality was not the sum of his differences from others, and that even the qualities that distinguished him were valuable chiefly because of all that united him with his fellows. At this time he drew up, in *The Story of a Novel*, a complete statement of his task as a Mythmaker:

The life of the artist at any epoch of man's history has not been an easy one. And here in America, it has often seemed to me, it may well be the hardest life that man has ever known. I am not speaking of some frustration in our native life, some barrenness of spirit, some arid Philistinism which contends against the artist's life and which prevents his growth. I do not speak of these things because I do not put the same belief in them that I once did. I am speaking as I have tried to speak from first to last in the concrete terms of the artist's actual experience, of the nature of the physical task before him. It seems to me that the task is one whose physical proportions are vaster and more difficult here than in any other nation on the earth. It is not merely that in the cultures of Europe and of the Orient the American artist can find no antecedent scheme, no structural plan, no body of tradition that can give his own work the validity and truth that it must have. It is not merely that he must make somehow a new tradition for himself, derived from his own life and from the enormous space and energy of American life, the structure of his own design; it is not merely that he is confronted by these problems; it is even more than this, that the labor of a complete and whole articulation, the discovery of an entire universe and of a complete language, is the task that lies before him.

Such is the nature of the struggle to which henceforth our lives must be devoted. Out of the billion forms of America, out of the savage violence and the dense complexity of all its swarming life; from the unique and single substance of this land and life of ours, must we draw the power and energy of our own life, the articulation of our speech, the substance of our art.

This is a noteworthy statement of an epic intention. It points to Wolfe's most conspicuous achievement: no other American novelist has given so vivid, exhilarating a sense, in such rich, precise detail, of "the enormous space and energy of American life." But if the statement is admirably sober for Wolfe, it still needs some qualification, and not merely to make room for other, more modest intentions. Characteristically, he magnifies the "physical task," the necessity of comprehending a "billion forms." The great American novel need not contain all of America, and in this respect is not clearly harder to write than a great Russian or English novel; Wolfe's own narrative, like his first-hand knowledge at the time, was largely confined to a few states in the East and South, yet it was adequate for his large purposes. Likewise he exaggerates the intellectual task of the American artist, who cannot draw on European culture, who must "make a new tradition for himself." Modern America is not so entirely new and unique, the American mythmaker is not clearly obliged to discover and create for himself an entire universe—and indeed had better not try to. The great myths of the past were not such conscious creations; they drew on deep, unconscious sentiment, emotion and desire, the common heritage that is indeed a commonwealth. Today such materials have to be discounted, supplemented, complicated, adapted—but they are still available. Wolfe himself had been drawing heavily on them. And as he finally began to make out the image he sought, the "strength and wisdom external to his need," it turned out to be an ancient image. He came out of his confusion precisely by becoming conscious of his heritage, of a "body of tradition" characteristically American but also rooted in an ancient European tradition.

"O lost!" he had exclaimed at the beginning, in lyrical anguish. At the end he declared, in sober prose, "I believe that we are lost here in America"; but he added, "I believe we shall be found." He summed up all he had learned in a symbolic refrain: "You can't go home again." He couldn't go back to his hometown, to art for glory's sake, to youthful dreams of fame, romantic love, or escape in foreign lands. Neither could any American artist go back to the ivory tower, to dreams of the charming past, to bohemian Europe, or to a snug Connecticut farmhouse (with modern improvements). Neither could America go back to normalcy, to the good old days of blind and brutal grab, to a complacent faith in Progress as defined by industrialists and ballyhooed by salesmen—to any easy, comfortable solution, any mere appeasement of the enemies without or within. Nevertheless in the deepest sense Wolfe had gone home again. His image is the great national myth, the American Dream.

This is the image of America as in fact a New World, where man can at last realize his hope of creating a great and good society, an everlasting New Deal with freedom and justice for all. It is an ancient type of tribal myth, in its concept of a unique origin and a unique destiny, but it was inspired more immediately by the natural potentialities of a vast continent, by the pioneering spirit of the frontiersmen, by the democratic ideals of the eighteenth century Enlightenment, by the modern myth of progress. It appears as the background of many folk legends and tall tales; as a political creed, embodied in the life and

11

work of Franklin, Jefferson, Jackson and Lincoln; as a poetic and religious image in the work of Whitman, Emerson and the Transcendentalists; as a philosophical faith in William James and John Dewey. It has also taken many crude forms, of naive optimism, noisy chauvinism, brawling individualism, vulgar materialism. It remains a living tradition because it has always had to fight for its life, especially against the mythology of big business. If the constant struggle for the realization of the dream is not, as Vernon Parrington conceived it, the central theme of American history (and Wolfe's conception is often close to Parrington's), it is at least a major theme. In recent years it has provided the explicit terms of the national drama, with such protagonists as Franklin Roosevelt and Henry Wallace—mythological heroes to some, mythological monsters to others; and the drama has moved to the world stage.

It is accordingly difficult to talk coolly about the national myth today. God bless America; but we are often embarrassed by a patriotic and moral fervor that obscures the primary responsibilities of writers. We have such depressing examples of wholesale wholesomeness as Van Wyck Brooks, Bernard DeVoto, and Howard Mumford Jones, whose approach to modern literature suggests an investigation by the F.B.I. And so we have to rehearse the elementary. The great national myth remains a myth; it has no absolute validity and is not necessarily the "true" meaning of American life. Neither is it the necessary base or frame for all genuine American literature, much less a guarantee of sound literature. A creative writer must finally be judged by the concrete experience he renders, not the abstract ideas he invokes; he must always remain true to his own perception and felt experience, guard against pretending to a knowledge and belief that as a citizen he perhaps ought to have but as an artist does not have; and if his thought and feeling do unite in the national myth, he has still to create his own subject matter, language, design. As for Wolfe, the conclusion he reached does not *ipso facto* make him a greater novelist. Moreover, he barely reached it. His final testament is a bald statement, the outline and not the full body of a mythology. It does not give his entire work a firm structure or a neat shape; it is not the triumphant resolution of a grand symphony.

Yet having said this, we may add that many literary men have been too easily embarrassed by moral and patriotic fervor, too self-conscious of their dignity as literary men rather than as men. Today some are too fearful of "literary nationalism," as if it were necessarily provincial or undignified; though at the same time they may proudly take their stand on the Old South or some other regional tradition. At any rate, nationalism is an old tradition in literature, and the American myth is not an arbitrary substitute for the Muse. It is a living tradition, with a rich mythology, readily available for literary purposes. It is grounded in the national consciousness over three centuries of history. It is not merely local and temporal, for it is grounded as well in the history of Europe, the ancient humanistic tradition. As for Wolfe, to repeat, his final testament is not the crowning spire of a massive design; but neither is it simply an intellectual postscript. It is an honest ending, because a natural culmination of his growth to maturity, a natural fulfillment of all his thought

13

and feeling. If, as he left it, it is a bare statement, the language and the concrete substance to body it out are implicit in all his novels.

2

Since the myth involves us in such large issues, we had better pause again and look more closely at the whole concept. Contemporaries have been at once gallant and humble in adopting this old word, with all its poor relations, its connotations of "primitive" or "merely fanciful," and in thus admitting the limits of their knowledge and their sophistication. Unfortunately, however, it remains a dangerously ambiguous word; and the brave or pious talk has also been pretty loose. A myth may be mythical in the less agreeable sense, the imaginative scheme may be largely imaginary. The myth is indispensable to civilization; but let us add at once that its most eloquent, whole-hearted, effective disciple in our time has been Adolf Hitler. Too many literary men have been blurring these important distinctions. Some, like Allen Tate, have adopted the old term chiefly as a means of putting science in its place, reasserting the superiority of the "imaginative truth" of poetry. Others, like Waldo Frank, have worshipped the myth as a mysterious symbol or agent of a still higher kind of truth, beyond the reach of reason—the "organic real," the "mystic truth." In this realm anything goes, and a Hitler may go best. So we had better return to "the facts of ordinary life" included in Schorer's definition. We need a "large, controlling image"; but we need as well some rational criterion, that we may not be blindly con-

14

trolled. We have to judge the myth by its coherence, its scope, its relevance, its adequacy—its ability to accommodate at once our ancient emotional needs and the terms of our new knowledge and experience.

By this criterion, Wolfe's version of the native myth is both comprehensive and realistic. Few contemporaries have sized up so wide a range of experience, or given to modern life a philosophical meaning that may more completely engage our powers of knowing, feeling and striving. Many lesser writers, content to work with folk or regional traditions, have achieved their limited intention; we may best appreciate their modest success by realizing that it is modest. Of the more ambitious efforts to seek the frame of a whole mythology, Mann's Joseph story is the most impressive achievement. Although it is rather remote from our immediate experience, despite Mann's use of Freudian symbolism, it does penetrate to the "timeless schema" underlying our experience, where life is "quotation" and eternal anniversary. But far less satisfying were the extraordinary efforts of two of our most remarkable writers—Yeats and Joyce. In his *Vision*, Yeats constructed a whole elaborate, occult mythology, replete with Masks, Wills, Bodies of Fate, Demons, etc.; in *Ulysses* and especially in *Finnegans Wake*, Joyce synthesized scores of old myths to express a vision that critics are still busy deciphering. Both schemes are arbitrary and synthetic, neither is generally usable. To enjoy the later poetry of Yeats, for example, most readers have to forget his mythology or at least refuse to take it seriously, regarding it much as they do the supernatural machinery of the old epic. Indeed, some literary devotees of the myth tell us that we

15

should not take seriously the ideas and beliefs expressed in poetry, and violently object to the "Doctrine of Relevance" in criticism. It appears that poetic myths should merely be dreamed over, not used for our living purposes.

Wolfe, however, took his myth altogether seriously—as he had to if only because he himself lived it. "We shall be found," he concluded; though just where and how he does not say. His testament is typically American in that it remains in the "optative mood," which Emerson remarked as the sign of our spiritual history. Yet Wolfe thoroughly earned his belief, by painful experience, during times that made the myth of progress seem simply mythical, and the American dream a mockery. He did not come by it through disillusionment or on the rebound from Marxism, as did others—such as Dos Passos—who have made a similar pilgrimage to native shrines; he had never put his faith in guaranteed solutions. At the same time, he was more realistic than Parrington; although he offered no specific program, he saw more clearly than Parrington that the ideals of Jeffersonian democracy had to be adapted to the new conditions of a complex industrial society, and the ancient enemy fought on new grounds. Altogether, his vision embraced the political and economic realities that have become increasingly important in modern civilization, conditioning all other interests and activities; while it remains more humane than such scientific or pseudo-scientific schemes as the orthodox Marxist myth, which is clearly relevant but also crude, narrow and harsh in its contempt of ancient values and its claim to unvarnished truth.

Wolfe can accordingly bear comparison with such eminent literary forebears as Emerson and Whitman. Their cheerful yea-saying was essentially temperamental, at times almost absent-minded; it too easily became a habit because they had too little sense of evil, or specifically of the evils that were growing as the "robber barons" corrupted their doctrine of individualism. Wolfe's affirmation was more genuinely philosophical. He was all too conscious of evil, not only because the depression forced social evils upon his attention, but because he had the tragic sense of life. Like the great tragic poets, he came to terms with life by taking on its worst meanings, going through its worst possibilities.

In this aspect, Wolfe's mature view is best approached through another useful concept that critics of modern poetry have been making much of—the method of irony. Like the metaphysical poets of the seventeenth century, contemporaries have been deliberately complicating the poetic experience, introducing diverse and discordant elements, setting up resistances and tensions, stressing ambiguities and incongruities, refusing to surrender unconditionally to any emotion or idea. In this way, Cleanth Brooks points out, the poet can guarantee the maturity of his poem by assimilating the actual complexities and discords of modern experience; he not only gives the poem dramatic conflict but earns his happy ending, and thereby makes it invulnerable to ironic contemplation. Whereas romantic poetry, with its oversimplified statements, requires a sympathetic audience to provide a sympathetic context, metaphysical poetry "can never be thrown, raw and naked, into a new context in which it may appear foolish and ridiculous."

This is indeed the method and the triumph of Shakespeare and Donne. The triumph of some contemporaries, however, is not so clear. Brooks usually considers only their technique, not the attitudes underlying the outward show. *The Waste Land*, for example, is dense and intricate with ironies that he admires; yet the outcome of this elaborate show is a very simple idea of the modern world, a view of unqualified waste, sordidness, futility—a view that to many readers seems pretty crude, oversimplified, even sentimental. Eliot also requires a sympathetic audience, not to say a patient one. And in this perspective Wolfe is not so foolish as he may at first appear.

Plainly, he can look pretty raw and naked. Often he lets go, passionately committing himself to ecstasy or to despair. Often, too, he indulges in a self-conscious, labored irony that is no less romantic; in his early work it may appear as a youthful thrilling over the Irony of Fate, at worst as a youthful cynicism. Yet underlying all these excesses was a genuine, tough-minded, ironic awareness, the bedrock of the tragic view of life. He had a deep sense of the essential incongruities of man's life on earth, the perpetual disquiet that is also the dignity of the human spirit, the inevitable end of the endless seeking. He constantly dwelt on the incongruities of America, a land fabulous in its immensity and its emptiness, its exultant magnificence and its desolating ugliness, its childlike innocence and its savage violence, its swarming busyness and its searing loneliness. In particular, Wolfe dwelt on the incongruities in human character. From Mr. Brill, a "lewd and innocent man" who pokes his head in for a few pages, to the gross, preposterous and grand figure of old Gant, the hero's father, his people are typically bundles of contradictions.

18

This consistent stress on the apparently inconsistent, which links him with such novelists as Dostoyevsky, Proust and Gide, is most marked in his great characters and scenes, and gives them their peculiar Gothic quality. The supreme example is the scene of the death of his brother Ben in *Look Homeward, Angel,* when, through pettiness, confusion, rancor, fury and horror, the Gant family draw together "in a superb communion of love and valiance."

No doubt Wolfe overdoes this grotesquerie, as he does everything else. A more serious fault, however, is the uncertainty of his attitude in his early work. At times the inconsistencies are not so much in his characters as in his wavering view of them. The Gants may become almost intolerable on occasion, not because Wolfe was deliberately shifting his emphasis to their mad blood, but because he was at the mercy of his own mad blood, writing in a surge of personal bitterness. Similarly his view of New York, of the South, of America, or of life in general was distorted by revulsions in mood. He tended to violent alternations, committing himself unconditionally now to wonder or joy, now to fury or despair. In short, Wolfe was keenly aware of the incongruities of human life, but he had yet to see them steadily and whole, to accept them as natural, to become reconciled to them—to embrace all the ironies in a consistently ironic attitude.

In time, however, his feeling became more impersonal, his vision steadier, his hold firmer. What had been a haunting sense of incongruity, a matter of feeling, became an intellectual grasp, a matter of philosophy. He came to see at once the good and the evil, and the good-in-evil; he

19

could view with wonder but without fury the inevitable contradictions of man, half-god and half-beast, whose joy is rooted in sorrow, whose glory is also his misery; he could care and not care that the best and the worst man can know are inseparably interwoven. He had risen to the double vision, the strength and wisdom of the tragic view of life. It is therefore not the only strength or the whole wisdom; Wolfe himself could say that the way of Christ was better than his own way, though he could never make it his own. But such humility is also a sign of the tragic wisdom. At least this vision gives dignity to his myth, even as it qualifies his final prophecy, for it links the history and destiny of America with the "tragic dignity" of human history as conceived by great poets and philosophers through the ages.

In the following chapters this broad outline of Wolfe's development will be filled out in detail. It will also be modified. His serious faults must be dwelt on, especially because they too are rooted in native traditions. It is doubtful that Wolfe ever would have become a skilled craftsman, or even a strictly professional writer. It is doubtful, moreover, that his best work lay before him when death cut short his career. In *The Hills Beyond*, a long fragment of a novel, we have a sample of his last writing. Here we see the new, sober, impersonal Wolfe, who is conscientiously practicing restraint, who has profited by criticism; and we must add, regrettably, that the gains are outweighed by a considerable loss in natural wealth and power. It is a respectable performance, but it does not look like a potential masterpiece. Even as we appreciate his growth to maturity we must add that it did not mean a steady enrichment of his art. His best novel remains his first—*Look Homeward, Angel.*

The conclusion of all this, I should say, is that the method of irony is even more appropriate for criticism than for poetry, since criticism must deal with the incongruities of literature as well as of life; and Wolfe provides an excellent text for illustrating this moral. Because the brilliant, original criticism that distinguishes this age is characteristically proud and exclusive, it is apt to become rather naive. Critics who closely analyze the method of irony in poetry may also have an oversimplified view of life and letters—oversimplified, paradoxically, in that they leave out the simplicities, the primary values and the ultimate uses of literature. Hence judgments of Wolfe's work, for all its obviousness, have seldom been decently balanced. While the simpler reviewers have patriotically rhapsodized over his powers, more acute critics have too perfunctorily noted and discounted these powers. Plainly, he requires a sympathetic audience. But so, in the final analysis, do all the acknowledged masters of fiction. To get at the great Victorians, for example, we have to put up with a great deal of sprawl, puppetry, mechanical plotting and shameless sentimentality. They can be made to look pretty raw and naked if thrown into the context, say, of Henry James; although what unsympathetic critics have done to James himself is still more inhumane. Similarly with Fielding, Sterne, Flaubert, Zola, Melville, Hardy, Dostoyevsky, Proust. How much one makes of their limitations and their excesses depends not only on fine critical intelligence but on temperament and critical fashion.

Specifically, Wolfe's reputation has suffered from the

current reaction against Romanticism and the current pre-occupation with esthetic form. He was indeed excessively romantic, in the broad sense of the word, and can be fitted into most of the innumerable specialized definitions. Nevertheless his romanticism is not simply a temporary aberration. Like that of the greater Romantic poets, it is rooted in a primary, permanent impulse of art, the impulse to freedom and abundance; and he can also be fitted into a more agreeable definition, placed in the widespread movement against a literal, earthbound realism toward a vital synthesis of "richness and reality." Likewise his sins as an artist, upon which it is easy to exercise irony, need to be viewed at a further ironic remove. In their very proper concern for the formal properties that distinguish literature as literature, critics have grown so fastidious that they tend to forget the primal qualities that distinguish great literature. Thus T. S. Eliot and R. P. Blackmur remark casually the "profound failure" of *Hamlet*. "Magnitude," Blackmur has said in discussing the art of fiction, "comes only with a completely realized technique, and what matures in a rational imagination is exactly that technique." By this standard it is hard to measure or explain the apparent magnitude of *Vanity Fair* or *War and Peace* (in fact, Blackmur has also called *War and Peace* a profound failure), or to grant Wolfe any magnitude worth speaking of. Nevertheless I believe that Wolfe does have it, and that somehow we must speak of it.

2. THE LEGEND OF A MAN'S HUNGER IN HIS YOUTH

LOOK HOMEWARD, ANGEL (1929) IS THE PORTRAIT OF THE artist as a child and a very young man. It carries Eugene Gant through school and college; its setting is the town of Altamont, in the mountains of western Catawba, and then the State University at Pulpit Hill. The leading characters are the members of Eugene's immediate family, in particular his father and his mother, his sister Helen, his brothers Luke and Ben. It is a chaotic household always united by fierce loyalties and a common heritage of furious vitality and lust for life, a compact household always torn by ugly dissension and a common destiny of loneliness and frustration, in which Eugene, the youngest child, is the pampered darling and the ugly duckling, petted, resented, admired, mocked, and never understood—except, perhaps, by his brother Ben, a lonely stranger like himself. Eugene's inner life, of course, is exceptional; it seems more so because the child is given much the same thoughts and passions as the young man (who in turn continues much the same for a long time after he has supposedly become an adult). The basic patterns of his youthful experience, however, are typical, including the familiar themes of growing pains, the discovery of an opposite sex, the discovery of the glorious world of books and the desire to escape into a larger, freer world. The climax of the novel is the death of Ben. The book ends with a conversation between Eugene and the spirit of Ben, still lonely and fiercely gentle. "A stone, a leaf, a door"—shall Eugene find them? Ben does not answer. "O lost, and by the wind grieved, ghost, come back again."

Of Time and the River (1935), "A Legend of Man's Hunger in His Youth," tells the story of the struggling young writer on his own, and the discovery that the really serious problems begin when a man is free. Escaped from his family, Eugene enters new worlds: at Harvard, where he takes Professor Hatcher's famous course in playwriting; in New York, where he becomes a college instructor; in Europe, where he travels restlessly. Everywhere he is still haunted by his family, blessed and cursed by his heritage, acutely conscious that he is "a man six feet six . . . in a world of five feet eight." Everywhere he is driven by his mad hunger, physical and spiritual, to devour the earth. "He would get up in the middle of the night to scrawl down insane catalogs of all that he had seen and done:—the number of books he had read, the number of miles he had travelled, the number of people he had known, the number of women he had slept with, the number of meals he had eaten, the number of towns he had visited, the number of states he had been in." Then he would make enormous catalogs of all the books, food, women, towns, and states that were left. Nevertheless, in the course of some nine hundred pages, he manages to meet a host of memorable people, from the elegant Francis Starwick of Harvard to Abe Jones of the East Side, and to devour, if not always to digest, a vast deal of richly varied experience. The story ends, or rather stops, with his return to America. On shipboard he meets a beautiful woman named Esther, and there are hints of a grand passion.

Bitterly as Wolfe resented the remark, it must be insisted at once that these novels are literally autobiographical. Naturally he omitted, altered, or fused many details; inevitably he colored or transfigured; but the liberties he took are so obvious or unimportant that it is hardly profitable to study the differences between the story of Eugene Gant and the life of Thomas Wolfe. For an adequate biographical sketch we need only change the names and add some dates. Wolfe was born on October 3, 1900. (The date inscribed on the watch Ben gave Eugene on his twelfth birthday is October 3, 1912.) *Look Homeward, Angel* covers his life to 1920, *Of Time and the River* from 1920 to 1925. Altamont, Catawba, is Asheville, North Carolina; the State University at Pulpit Hill is the University of North Carolina at Chapel Hill, where Wolfe received his A.B. in 1920; Professor Hatcher's famous course in playwriting at Harvard is Professor Baker's famous course, and Wolfe's first literary efforts were in the drama (a remarkably uncongenial form for him); the university in which Eugene taught is New York University, with which Wolfe was connected from 1924 to 1930. All the important characters in the novels are drawn straight from his life. He apparently found it difficult to change even the names of those who had meant most to him: his father, W. O. Wolfe, becomes W. O. Gant; his mother, Julia Elizabeth, becomes Eliza; and his brother Ben remains Ben.[1] The important events of his later life also get into his later novels. For the present it is enough to add that after 1930, when he left New York University on a Guggenheim Fellowship, he devoted all his working time to writing. He died on September 15, 1938.

Now, one may grant Wolfe that all serious fiction is autobiographical, in that it is written out of the author's deepest experience. Nevertheless one must add that hardly any other novelist has used his own experience so directly and so exclusively. On his first trip to Europe, Wolfe kept assuring his mother that he was "writing it all up." He was always writing up his history, and then worrying over the problem of how to fit it all into his novels. Edward C. Aswell, his last editor, remarks that he was amazed to find, after he had removed all the extraneous matter, that the rest of the manuscript fell into a perfect shape, and that all Wolfe's novels together become in effect "one book"; he describes this "unity" as an "extraordinary literary achieve-

[1] He had similar difficulty with many minor details. To illustrate, Eugene travels out of Altamont on Pullman K-19—and on K-19 his family rode when they brought Wolfe back to Asheville, in death; it was one of the Pullmans regularly assigned to the Asheville run. Likewise he was apt to make slips in his efforts to disguise. Eugene and his friend Starwick have a favorite restaurant in Boston known on p. 276 as Posillipo's; on p. 317 it becomes Masillippo's. But a slip that shocked some critics—an occasional shift from "Eugene" to "I"—is not so unpardonable a give-away as they made out. The entire novel was originally written in the first person.

26

ment." There is indeed a unity. But aside from the fact that Aswell had to remove the extraneous matter himself, this is scarcely extraordinary, nor is it strictly a *literary* achievement. The unity is primarily that of a life, a personality. It might almost be reduced to the statement that all of Wolfe's work was written by Wolfe, and chiefly about Wolfe; it might be found as well in the volume of his letters to his mother.

I should not insist upon this distinction merely out of a desire to be scrupulous or conscientiously critical. The issue here is not the academic question of whether Wolfe's sprawling books are "really" novels at all; it is not a matter of definition, of failure to disguise his materials or to get them into a conventional form. Rather, it is Wolfe's prolonged inability to dominate his materials, to master any kind of form. This inability either to escape or to command his own life history is the immediate sign and source of his faults as an artist. They are grievous faults, as he himself admitted; they are also typically American, and symptomatic of an age of disorder; they are finally the measure of his growth, as the index of all he had to outgrow. On all counts they need to be seen clearly for what they are, and not dressed up as qualities of his original genius. In simple kindness as well as justice to Wolfe, it is well to begin by saying the worst.

The notorious diffuseness of his lengthy novels is accordingly quite different from the sprawl of Balzac, Dickens, Zola, Melville, or Tolstoy. It is due in part to his youthful obsession with sheer quantity or extent of experience, and his youthful passion for "expressing it all"—everything must be told, nothing implied. More significantly, it is due

27

to the absence of a clear intention or design. The old masters were careless, but they were seldom confused; they could be leisurely and digress freely because they knew where they were going, had something to digress from. Wolfe, on the other hand, always felt swamped by his material, because of his teeming memory. He conceived his main problem as not how to select, to shape, but how to get it all in, to let it flow freely. Hence he got far too much in, and despite all his anguish it flowed much too freely, because his memory was in fact teeming.

Often Wolfe includes an episode merely because it happened so, and dwells on it because his memories are especially bright. In *Of Time and the River*, for example, he gives some hundred pages to the wealthy Pierce family, with a lovingly detailed rendition of their world of luxury, power and ease. The episode has a point: Wolfe at first is dazzled by this world, then inevitably disappointed in it. But this point is obvious long before he is done, it will be made many times again, and meanwhile Wolfe is much more dazzled and disappointed by the elegant Pierces than his readers are. Similarly he includes some twenty pages of his travel diary, jottings that are at best the raw material of fiction; somehow he must get in all his impressions of France. When he was dissatisfied or forced to edit, his first impulse was to write more rather than to cut or revise. For he had no frame of reference, no clear criterion by which to determine relevance. He had, in short, no specific *artistic* purpose.

In a youthful letter to his mother, Wolfe expressed his simple creed. His work is to be "true and honest and courageous, and the rest doesn't matter . . . it is life, life,

28

life—the only thing that matters." So it is—finally. But to life everything is relevant, and art does not begin until there is a limited purpose, a decision of just what matters for the work in hand. Nor can we defend Wolfe, as Edward Aswell loyally attempts to do, by inventing for him "special kinds of form," which come down to the ways in which "things happen in real life." On this principle anything would go; and in any event Wolfe never did originate a new kind of form or technique, nor were his materials so original or unconventional as to call for one. When Aswell goes on to attack the "academic minds" that insist that "an artist should improve on life," he only makes explicit the pathetic fallacy of realism. It is precisely the business of the artist to improve on life, else he would have no business at all. He has literally to compose, to give life a shape and meaning that in its mere flow it does not have; which is not to say, of course, necessarily a pretty shape or edifying meaning. The best case for Wolfe is that in many separate episodes he did improve on life magnificently, and that altogether he finally succeeded in getting a great deal of life into some kind of shape.

Although Wolfe's indiscriminate devotion to "real life" was most obviously associated with the realistic movement, it was also one of the dubious elements of his American heritage. In an essay "In Dispraise of Life, Reality, and Experience," Morris Cohen has deplored the tendency in American philosophy (especially in William James) to make these terms honorific, and in their name to condone any sacrifice of logical rigor. American literature is similarly marked by an indifference to form, technique, the rigors of artistry. "No one will get at my verses," Whitman announced, "who insists upon viewing them as literary performances"; literature would cramp his style. "Who cares for fine style!" exclaimed Frank Norris. "Tell your yarn and let your style go to the devil. We don't want literature, we want life." This is the democratic spirit, careless or scornful of forms; but it was intensified by the frontier spirit, the folk tradition of tall tale, monologue, rhapsody, declamation and burlesque. Thus our most conscious and careful artists, such as Hawthorne, Poe and Henry James, have typically been remote from the people. Our most characteristically American writers—Whitman, Emerson, Thoreau, Mark Twain—have used the popular forms or modes. As Constance Rourke pointed out in her *American Humor*, their work has a pervasive air of improvisation: they do not compose—they soliloquize, they rhapsodize, they spin yarns. Likewise Wolfe, who had the native tradition in his blood, wrote by ear. He was a mighty talker and a natural mimic; his friends report that he often talked lustily and at length about some happening, in much the same words that he would later use in his novels. He thought of all his novels as one "book," and this book was an improvisation on a grand scale.[2]

[2] In the light of this tradition, perhaps the most thoroughly American of living writers is Henry Miller, who was long an expatriate and is now pleased to regard this country as an "air-conditioned nightmare," a huge cesspool, a slaughter house, etc. His *Tropic of Cancer* and *Tropic of Capricorn* are extraordinary mélanges of tall tale, rhapsody, monologue, burlesque, extravaganza—folk forms in ultra-modern dress. Miller is still devoted to the image of the romantic artist, and is like the early Wolfe in his immense energy and appetite, his often grotesque characterization, his indifference to form, and his headlong excess. On different grounds he has the same intoxicated passion for LIFE and REALITY (the capitals are his own).

A more particular reason for his excesses, however, was the romantic concept, also sanctioned by Emerson, Whitman and Thoreau, that a poet's intuition finds its appropriate expression naturally, spontaneously, as a plant grows. The young Wolfe was by no means indifferent to fine style—if anything, he liked it too fine. But in his self-absorption he assumed that intense emotion generates its own adequate form, and that complete self-expression automatically becomes full communication. Hence he often quit his specific job as a novelist for the sake of a direct expression of his emotions, substituting rhetoric for concrete representation. He declaimed, he wrote prose poems, he chanted. He brought back the tradition of oratory, which is the oldest American literary tradition.

I should not attempt to pass a final judgment on such rhetoric; the history of literature appears to indicate that verdicts are largely dictated by fashion and personal taste, not by eternal principles of prose. Neither should I make a law of the current doctrine, stemming from Flaubert, that a novelist must keep out of his story and allow it to make its own point. Although I prefer to have the meanings dramatized, presented in terms of fiction rather than of essay, the great novelists of the past who talked so freely about their stories are usually worth listening to; the advantage of the novel form over the drama lies precisely in its breadth and freedom; and mythmakers might well be granted this freedom to amplify and heighten the meanings of their fable. It is difficult to deny the eloquence of Wolfe's best passages in this rhetorical kind. A collection of them has been published in a separate volume, *The*

Face of a Nation, which might stand on the same shelf with *Leaves of Grass.*

Yet this collection also makes clear how easily these passages can be detached from the novels, and why they grow monotonous. Wolfe endlessly repeats, not only his favorite themes but his favorite phrases—the "bitter briefness of our days," the "brutal stupefaction of the streets," etc. He may be deliberately stressing a *leitmotif,* but he may seem simply drunk on his own eloquence. Moreover, his naturally rhythmical prose can become almost metrical, his music a sing-song beat. Some passages might be scanned: "All this has been upon the earth, and will abide forever. But you are gone; our lives are ruined and broken in the night, our lives are mined below us by the river, our lives are whirled away into the sea and darkness, and we are lost unless you come to give us life again." In general, rhythm and resonance are the most conspicuous qualities of Wolfe's lyrical passages, and they tend to involve not only repetition and wordiness but a sacrifice of precision. In *A Stone, A Leaf, A Door,* John S. Barnes has arranged some of these passages in the form of free verse, with a good ear for their rhythmical patterns. In this form they appear more obviously lyrical, but at times they also appear thin in texture; a phrase that completes the rhythmical pattern may have little meaning or value in itself. Here, for example, is a stanza from the prose-poem which introduces *Look Homeward, Angel:*

> Naked and alone we came into exile.
> In her dark womb
> We did not know our mother's face;

LEGEND OF A MAN'S HUNGER IN YOUTH

> From the prison of her flesh have we come
> Into the unspeakable and incommunicable prison
> Of this earth.

The many unaccented syllables in the penultimate line are rhythmically effective in that they accelerate the pace as the stanza approaches its climax, and emphasize the idea of an earthly fate too dark and disordered to be expressed in measured words. But "unspeakable" and "incommunicable" are not very apt or precise adjectives here; the "prison" that is rhythmically contrasted with the prison of the mother's womb (in itself a dubious metaphor) is inconsistent with the previous metaphor of "exile"; and one may question whether the concluding rhythmical unit, "Of this earth," deserves the emphasis it gets.

All taste aside, one may make an objective distinction in Wolfe's rhetoric. There are passages in which emotion is built up out of sharp, concrete images, the dramatic material of a scene. There are other passages in which a ready-made emotion is merely asserted, or invoked by vague, unlocalized images that, in Blackmur's phrase, "can be used like postage stamps on anybody's mail." [3] Wolfe is much too prone to invoke instead of to render, to tell us what to feel instead of building the feeling, and to be carried away by a train of feeling started off by mere habit or verbal association instead of by fresh perception. Even apart from the stereotyped rhythms and images, and from

[3] Perhaps the most unflattering comment on Wolfe's poetry was offered by a large advertising firm to whom he showed the manuscript of *Look Homeward, Angel*. They tried to sign him up for three years as an advertising copywriter, promising him big money.

the too fancy feathers in his cap, his habit of deserting his characters is another sign of self-indulgence, lack of fidelity to his main task as a novelist.

This undisciplined self-expression is the more conspicuous because it is such a tumultuous, violent, extravagantly emotional self that Wolfe is expressing; and so we have to put up with the notorious excesses of Eugene Gant. Eugene is forever beside himself, which is where he wants to be. He "yells," "howls," "bellows madly," "snarls like a wild beast"; he is repeatedly "choked with fury," "white with constricted rage," "frantic with horror"; when he broods in silence it is to contemplate things "intolerable," "implacable," "unutterable"; when he nevertheless utters the unutterable, his favorite adjectives are "wild," "tortured," "demented," "demonic," "maniacal"; and at the end of such bouts with himself or the world, he "beats his knuckles bloody on the stamped-out walls." Extensive quotation is needless and depressing; one passage will give the idea:

Now a huge, naked, and intolerable shame and horror pressed down on Eugene with a crushing and palpable weight out of the wet, gray skies of autumn. The hideous gray stuff filled him from brain to bowels, was everywhere and in everything about him so that he breathed it out of the air, felt it like a naked stare from walls and houses and the faces of the people, tasted it on his lips, and endured it in the screaming and sickened dissonance of ten thousand writhing nerves so that he could no longer sit, rest, or find oblivion, exhaustion, forgetfulness or repose anywhere he went, or release from the wild unrest that drove him constantly about. . . . He saw the whole earth with the sick eyes, the sick heart, the sick flesh, and writhing nerves of this gray accursed weight of shame and horror in which his life lay drowned, and from which it seemed he could never more emerge to know the

34

music of health and joy and power again; and from which, likewise, he could not die, but must live hideously and miserably the
rest of his days, like a man doomed to live forever in a state of
retching and abominable nausea of heart, brain, bowels, flesh and
spirit.

What has happened here is that Eugene has just received
his first rejection slip.

It is safe to say that all this is somewhat exaggerated.
Even without the testimony of Wolfe's friends, we would
guess that he experienced some mild emotions, uttered
some casual remarks, left some walls unbloodied. Likewise
we would discount some passages on the basis of simple
arithmetic. While at Harvard, Eugene reads like a mad-
man, "tearing the entrails" from 2,000 books a year ("deliberately the number is set low"); but a few pages later
we are told that he was also spending "thousands of good
hours" thinking about a certain waitress.[4] The more serious trouble, however, is that too much of all this is literally
true, and that Wolfe was not deliberately exaggerating for
effect. His faults may be summed up as a remorseless excess, but he had in fact been a very excessive young man.
He was still full of mixed emotions, some deep and brooding, others touchy or moody, but all boiling at the same
temperature. He was still more concerned with expressing
his emotion than with understanding it; or he hoped to

[4] Edward Aswell provides a slide rule for translating these round
numbers that Wolfe loved. Early in the summer before his death,
while on a journey through the West, Wolfe wrote to Aswell that
he already had 50,000 words of notes on his journey. But when
Wolfe said that he had written a million words he meant only "I
have written a lot"; Aswell explains that 50,000 meant "I have
just started." Thus his notes, when completed, turned out to be
fewer than 10,000 words.

35

come upon an understanding simply by overwriting. He felt the more intensely because he still did not know what to think.

Hence Wolfe is apt to be at his worst when he is alone with his hero, writing directly of the inner world in which presumably are to be found the important meanings of his life story. To many readers, Eugene Gant is the least interesting and least convincing of Wolfe's major characters. His rages and despairs become more tiresome because we seldom really see him; he is a disembodied passion, an incessant blaze and blare without shape or substance. And when the outer world is presented directly as he sees it, it may also take on a violent monotony and finally become unrecognizable. Here, for example, is Eugene's impression of New York in one of his black moods:

Around him in the streets, again, as winter came, he heard a million words of hate and death: a million words of snarl and sneer and empty threat, of foul mistrust and lying slander: already he had come to see the poisonous images of death and hatred in the lives of a million people—he saw with what corrupt and venomous joy they seized on every story of man's dishonor, defeat, or sorrow, with what vicious jibe and jeer they greeted any evidence of mercy, honesty, or love.

Of this, all one can say is that it isn't so.

Altogether, there is no question of Wolfe's passionate sincerity, his agonized effort to be utterly "true and honest and courageous." There is also no question that truth-telling is an even more arduous business than he at first conceived. If he often reveals more about himself than he intends, making an embarrassing show of his naïveté, he

36

often reveals considerably less than he intends, exposing but not elucidating. If he is being honest and courageous in exposing so much, he nevertheless finds it too easy to let go, to indulge in the luxury of all this passion; to forego this luxury would have cost him still more anguish. His limitations may be exposed most clearly on his own ground, by setting his novels beside such other autobiographical novels as *Sons and Lovers*, *Of Human Bondage*, *The Portrait of the Artist as a Young Man* and *Remembrance of Things Past*. In these the hero is a creation, not a *nom de plume*, and his life a work of art, not a flood of memories. In this company Wolfe appears a very artless young man.

2

"Genius is not enough," declared Bernard DeVoto, after a devastating review of Wolfe's sins as an artist. Genius is a great deal, however, and nothing can take its place; the intelligence, honesty, earnestness, and skill of our many good second-rate writers are not enough either. And this artless young man is indeed one of the few contemporaries who leave a strong impression of genius. No less obvious than Wolfe's sins are the powers that also make him stand out in the company where we left him.

To begin with, Wolfe had the virtues of his defects: the freshness and poignance of naïveté, the force and eloquence of passion, the abundance and energy of unrestraint, the resonance of rhetoric. His excesses were rooted in an excess of vitality. Hence all the main clauses of the indictment of his work may be subordinated, and at

37

least must be qualified. If his hunger for experience was insane, he was nevertheless able to assimilate a great deal. If his gospel of Life was a romantic passion, it was as well a discipline, the means of a saving honesty and humility. If his impulse to write instead of to cut blurred the shape of his novels, it also enriched their substance. Wolfe gave the immediate answer to his critics in a letter to F. Scott Fitzgerald:

You say that the great writer like Flaubert has consciously left out the stuff that Bill or Joe will come along presently and put in. Well, don't forget, Scott, that a great writer is not only a leaver-outer but also a putter-inner, and that Shakespeare and Cervantes and Dostoevsky were great putter-inners—greater putter-inners, in fact, than taker-outers and will be remembered for what they put in—remembered, I venture to say, as long as Monsieur Flaubert will be remembered for what he left out.

Wolfe's passion for putting in, moreover, was not pure self-indulgence. Because of his popular reputation for simply pouring out millions of words, and then depending on his editors to make a novel out of them, it needs to be emphasized that he subjected himself to a very arduous discipline. He spent a long apprenticeship in a disheartening effort to write plays, and learned to leave out enough so that he almost succeeded in reaching Broadway. He spent several years of hard work on *Look Homeward, Angel*, not merely in an effort to make it bigger. He then wrote a novel called *K-19*, about a train and the lives of the passengers who by chance were thrown together; but he agreed with his editor that it was not good enough to follow his first novel, and put it aside. After some four years of desperate work on *Of Time and the River*, he still

38

felt that it was not good enough either; this time his editor had almost to force him to publish it. "I am inevitable," he kept telling his mother in his youthful letters, "I have genius"; but this apparent egotism was also a high dedication, and made him humble about his actual achievement. In his letter to Fitzgerald he added that he was not arrogantly contemptuous of criticism: "One of my besetting sins, whether you know it or not, is a lack of confidence in what I do."

Such passion and such labor are in themselves, of course, not enough to make a major novelist. Neither is "genius" enough for critical purposes—the term is too large and vague to permit profitable discussion. But Wolfe had gifts that may be specified precisely enough for critical inspection. Most conspicuous is his remarkable sensory equipment. "The quality of my memory," he writes modestly in *The Story of a Novel*, "is characterized, I believe, in a more than ordinary degree by the intensity of its sense impressions, its power to evoke and bring back the odors, sounds, colors, shapes, and feel of things with concrete vividness." He goes on to tell how he would suddenly recall, while sitting in a café in Paris, the iron railing along the boardwalk in Atlantic City:

It was all so vivid and concrete that I could feel my hand upon it and know the exact dimensions, its size and weight and shape. . . . And this utterly familiar, common thing would suddenly be revealed to me with all the wonder with which we discover a thing which we have seen all our life and yet have never known before. Or again, it would be a bridge, the look of an old iron bridge across an American river, the sound the train makes as it goes across it; the spoke-and-hollow rumble of the ties below; the look of the muddy banks; the slow, thick, yellow wash of an

American river; an old flat-bottomed boat half filled with water stogged in the muddy bank; or it would be, most lonely and haunting of all the sounds I know, the sound of a milk wagon as it entered an American street just at the first gray of the morning, the slow and lonely clopping of the hoof upon the street, the jink of bottles, the sudden rattle of a battered old milk can, the swift and hurried footsteps of the milkman, and again the jink of bottles, a low word spoken to his horse, and then the great, slow, clopping hoof receding into silence, and then quietness and a bird song rising in the street again.

Wolfe did not merely pour out these memories, however. His immense labors were devoted above all to an effort to realize the "exactitudes" of his impressions. Through his hero he describes the puritanical rigors of his long apprenticeship:

In his effort to explore his experience, to extract the whole, essential truth of it, and to find a way to write about it, he sought to recapture every particle of the life he knew down to its minutest details. He spent weeks and months trying to put down on paper the exactitudes of countless fragments—what he called, "the dry, caked colors of America"—how the entrance to a subway looked, the design and webbing of the elevated structure, the look and feel of an iron rail, the particular shade of rusty green with which so many things are painted in America. Then he tried to pin down the foggy color of the brick of which so much of London is constructed, the look of an English doorway, of a French window, of the roofs and chimney pots of Paris, of a whole street in Munich —and each of these foreign things he then examined in contrast to its American equivalent.

These passages give the key to the richness and finally the soundness of Wolfe's art. He was able to keep his head because he stayed in his senses. He always had an uncommonly keen, strong sense of reality: of the immediacies of life as it is seen and felt, and through them of the permanencies of human desire and emotion. He knew the commonplace in all its wonder, beauty, strangeness and terror. Too often he merely catalogued, and too often indulged in a vague, emotional impressionism: but much more often he rendered, concretely and dramatically, with a wealth of precise detail that gives body and point to his emotion.

The difference is illustrated in the opening section of *Of Time and the River*. Eugene gets on the train to go North, and Wolfe, in his anxiety to tell all, gets some facts into the record:

The journey from the mountain town of Altamont to the tower-masted island of Manhattan is not, as journeys are conceived in America, a long one. The distance is somewhat more than 700 miles, the time required to make the journey a little more than twenty hours.

Then Eugene's emotions begin to rise, and Wolfe swings into one of his chants:

Who has seen fury riding in the mountains? Who has known fury striding in the storm? Who has been mad with fury in his youth, given no rest or peace or certitude by fury, driven on across the earth by fury, until the great vine of the heart was broke, the sinews wrenched, the little tenement of bone, blood, marrow, brain, and feeling in which great fury raged, was twisted, wrung, depleted, worn out, and exhausted by the fury which it could not lose or put away? Who has known fury, how it came?

This goes on for a page or so: we see nothing, we only hear a swelling noise, a flood of emotion that has swept away the scene while going nowhere in particular. But then Wolfe gets his eye on the object and settles down to his proper business. As the train slides through the night, we are given a sharply etched image of the "anomalous, shabby-ornate, inept, and pitifully pretentious" square of the typical American small town, haunting and lonely in its "ghastly imitation of swarming life and metropolitan gaiety . . . and the almost total absence of life itself":

> The lights burn, the electric signs wink and flash, the place is still horribly intact in all its bleak prognathous newness, but all the people are dead, gone, vanished. The place is a tomb of frozen silence, as terrifying in its empty bleakness as those advertising backdrops one saw formerly in theatres, where the splendid buildings, stores, and shops of a great street are painted in the richest and most flattering colors, and where there is no sign of life whatever.

Innumerable passages such as this contribute to the blazing pageantry of Wolfe's novels, by which he evokes, more vividly and fully than any other American writer, the look, sound and feel of American life: of the raw thrust of tank and factory, of the whistle-wail of trains at night and the baying of liners in the harbors, of rickety tenements beneath the webbing of great bridges, of red barns with the bright tatter of old circus posters, of hard, slangy, reckless, humorous voices in the swarming streets, of wasteland rust and rubbish—of all the immensely varied forms and substances, against the background of the wild, lyric, casual, savage, fecund earth. These passages, moreover, are not merely striking backdrops—they are the living stage, inseparable from the drama. They are the concrete substance of the American myth, whose central meaning Wolfe was seeking.

Similarly one reason why Wolfe's characters are so memorable is that they are so vividly seen. He had an ex-

cellent eye for the feature or gesture that instantly reveals
a personality. In a sentence he paints a striking Rembrandt
picture of old Gant, dying, wasted away except for his
huge, powerful hands:

> Thus, as he sat there now, staring dully out across the city, an
> emaciated and phantasmal shadow of a man, there was, in the
> appearance of these great living hands of power (one of which
> lay with an enormous passive grace and dignity across the arm of
> his chair and the other extended and clasped down upon the
> handle of a walking stick), something weirdly incongruous, as if
> the great strong hands had been unnaturally attached to the puny
> lifeless figure of a scarecrow.

And these still-living hands, hanging so grotesquely from
the scarecrow form of the old stone-cutter, evoke his whole
life, "the lost world . . . of manual power, hunger, fury,
savage abundance and wild joy, the whole enchanted
structure of that lost life of magic he had made for them."

Another sign of Wolfe's extraordinary sensory memory
is his rich dialogue. Accordingly his dialogue is not, like
Hemingway's, a brilliant creation; particularly in the
speech of his father and mother, Wolfe had the adventi-
tious benefit of remarkable originals.[5] He is also apt to re-
produce with tiresome literalness, or to accentuate crudely
the obvious manner or mannerism; we may regret his long
stay in New York after we overhear for the hundredth
time, "Naw, dat was duh otheh guy." At its best, however,
Wolfe's dialogue is a superb dramatic medium, realistic

---

[5] In his introduction to *Thomas Wolfe's Letters to His Mother*,
John Terry cites a few samples of Mrs. Wolfe's conversation, as
recorded by a dictaphone; and one instantly recognizes the voice
of Eliza Gant.

yet full of flavor. The flavor is richest in the family scenes, as when old Gant launches his preposterous tirades: "Merciful God! Why must this be put upon me in my old age?" But all his main characters have their own unmistakable accent; all are heard as distinctly as they are seen, and are known by their idiom.

What this comes down to is a natural gift for mimicry, and Wolfe's delight in it is typical of the American comic tradition. It has led some critics to praise him as a great satirist. Actually, his satire is limited and uneven, often amateurish. In *Look Homeward, Angel* he himself points to its limitations when he remarks that satire is a "high and subtle art," and "great satire needs the sustenance of great fable"; for subtlety is hardly his forte, and his fable is still cloudy. He will at times overdo an obvious caricature of an obvious subject, such as William Jennings Bryan. He is apt to be especially heavyhanded when he takes out his disillusionment on the wealthy, the sophisticated, the city-bred—these whom he envies even while he despises them. He again points to what he lacks when he speaks of the "great comic intelligence" that is in his family; for he still has too little of the detachment of the comic spirit, and his intellectual powers and interests are still sharply limited. What his family does have is a natural earthy humor, an immense gusto combined with a lively sense of the ridiculous, characterized particularly by the frontiersman's roaring delight in grotesque exaggeration. And it is this inheritance that most obviously inspires Wolfe's comic creations. Here, for example, is his famous Uncle Bascom:

Shortly before nine o'clock of every working-day he would emerge from a subway exit near the head of the street and pause

vaguely for a moment, making a craggy eddy in the tide of issuing
workers that foamed swiftly about him while he stood with his
enormous bony hands clutched comically before him at the waist,
as if holding himself in, at the same time making the most horrible
grimaces with his lean and amazingly flexible features. These
grimaces were made by squinting his small sharp eyes together,
widening his mouth in a ghastly travesty of a grin, and convolving
his chin and cheek in a rapid series of pursed lips and horrible
squints as he swiftly pressed his rubbery underlip against a few
enormous horse teeth that decorated his upper jaw. Having completed these facial evolutions, he glanced quickly and, it must be
supposed, blindly in every direction; for he then plunged heedlessly
across the street, sometimes choosing the moment when traffic had
been halted, and pedestrians were hurrying across, sometimes div-
ing into the midst of a roaring chaos of motor cars, trucks, and
wagons, through which he sometimes made his way in safety,
accompanied only by a scream of brake bands, a startled barking
of horns, and the hearty curses of frightened drivers, or from
which, howling with terror in the center of a web of traffic which
he had snarled hopelessly and brought to a complete standstill,
he was sometimes rescued by a red-faced and cursing young
Irishman who was on point duty at that corner.

But Uncle Bascom also leads to the deeper qualities of
Wolfe's art, the sense of not only the broadly ridiculous
but the profoundly incongruous. Although Wolfe's world
at first glance looks much like the world of Dickens or
Sinclair Lewis, his many eccentrics are not mere carica-
tures or satiric types. They are more complex and individualized, they present more facets, they have an inner life
and history—they can step out of their author's fantastic
world and go on living in the everyday world. Thus Uncle
Bascom enters like somebody out of Dickens, as impossible
and as irresistible; but presently we are not simply delighting in him. We have entered his own secret world, the

thought and feeling behind his ludicrous grimaces and howls, and are reading "the history of man's loneliness, his dignity, his grandeur and despair." We are reading, in other words, something more like Dostoyevsky than Dickens. And though the gusto and the humor that go with it are characteristically American, the whole blend cannot be matched in American literature.

In this constant stress upon incongruity, once more, is the peculiar quality of Wolfe's fiction. We get it in Abe Jones, gray, ugly, inept, dreary, "dully intellectual and joylessly poetic, his spirit gloomily engulfed in a great cloud of Yiddish murk"—yet a loyal friend, the salt of the earth, "a wonderfully good, rare, and high person." We get it in Francis Starwick, a much rarer spirit, brilliant, polished, yet corrupt in his fineness, possessing all gifts except the "one small grain of common earth that could have saved him," and bearing within him the seeds of an abominable doom. We get it above all in Eugene's immediate family. His sister Helen is barren, childless and pathless in her immense vitality, furious and often cruel in her immense generosity, driven blindly by a need to exhaust her inexhaustible energy in the service of others, a need to receive lavish praise for this service, and a need to feel that it has not been appreciated; and so she is indiscriminately lavish in kindness, affection and abuse, lashing out hysterically against the world or herself, forever frenzied in her pursuit of a peace and quiet that she could never endure. His mother, Eliza, is beetle-wise and beetle-blind, innocent and ignoble in her instinctive materialism, sacrificing her husband, her children and herself to her passion for accumulating property, the "insensate mythology of hoarding"; yet in all her pettiness and meanness she is indestructible, indomitable in her fortitude, her fidelity and her integrity, triumphant over sorrow, loss, age and all the ravages of time and chance. And his father, the "fallen Titan" who is the grandest figure in Wolfe's novels, is like Captain Ahab an "ungodly, godlike man," at once majestic, grotesque and pitiably human in his love of ritual and order and in the violent, foul disorder of his life; in the rich, absurd rhetoric swelling with the full tide of his humor, his fury, his piety and his chicanery; and in his desolation, the gray loneliness of a man of vivid senses and enormous gusto who is forever a stranger, known to his wife and to all the world only as "Mr. Gant."

I have already remarked that Wolfe tends to exaggerate such incongruities. He had a natural love of the grotesque, and as a young writer was prone to see everything twice its size. The serious fault, however, is not so much that his scenes are too highly colored as that the colors are not always balanced or blended. In his bitter moods he is apt to forget the incongruities, and magnify simply the ugliness in his family or his surroundings. We get quite different impressions of Eliza, for example. When Ben is dying, she bustles about eagerly, pathetically, for a terrible reason:

> She was not wanted in the sick-room; the dying boy did not want to see her. She had seen him turn his head wearily away when she had gone in. Behind her white face dwelt this horror, but she made no confession, no complaint. She bustled around doing useless things with an eager matter-of-factness. And Eugene, choked with exasperation at one moment, because of her heavy optimism, was blind with pity the next when he saw the terrible fear and pain in her dull black eyes.

This is true and good; here Wolfe is above both the exasperation and the pity. But in other scenes in *Look Homeward, Angel* he seems to be feeling only exasperation—and very seldom only pity. He seems to approve when Eugene thanks Eliza, as well as his whole family, for "the ten million hours of cruelty or indifference, and the thirty minutes of cheap advice."

Hence some critics have likewise stressed the spiritual poverty of Wolfe's background, and attributed his hunger for life to this poverty. They have pitied the young artist who so passionately wanted to belong to America, but who was denied the ordinary decencies of a home, of people to love, of anything to belong to, and who seldom met anything but suspicion, hostility, or at most good-natured contempt.

This is a shallow, sentimental view of Wolfe's early life, and finally an injustice to his work as well as to his family. If he had plenty to complain of, so do most sensitive youngsters; and he also had much to be grateful for. The environment that was in one aspect mean, harsh and barren was in another unusually rich. The mountains that shut him in a little world also exhilarated him, stirred a feeling for the immense, elemental, timeless world. Among all the townspeople who were standardized individualists of the bourgeois acquisitive school were also many genuine individuals in the old frontier tradition. Above all, Wolfe was fortunate in his immediate heritage. From his mother he got not only his remarkable memory but her inexhaustible memories, upon which he drew so heavily. From his father he got not only his gift for rhetoric and his hunger but abundant nourishment, as lavish a provision of poetry and humor as of food and drink. From both he got his deep feeling for the land and for the folk. "One half of me is great fields and mighty barns," he wrote his mother, "and one half of me is the great hills of North Carolina." The excessiveness of his whole family, the fierce dissension from which he suffered, sprang from the full-blooded energy, vitality and lust for life that he also inherited.

At least Wolfe's early life in a community of hill folk provided him with richer materials than he ever managed to extract from his later travels in the wide world. If it was not a congenial home, a home the mature artist could go back to, neither was it one that had to be utterly disowned or outgrown. What Wolfe more especially needed to outgrow was his excessive bitterness, the impertinence and unwisdom of simply regretting his early experience. For his occasional indulgence of this bitterness obscured his own intentions in *Look Homeward, Angel*. He was genuinely surprised and pained by the uproar its publication caused in Asheville; if he had not tried to spare his neighbors, he had not thought that he was writing an exposé. In particular he had wanted to stress the qualities of greatness in his family. In a telegram to his sister "Helen," [6] thanking her for a kind comment on the novel, he declared repeatedly that his leading characters are "fine people," "grand people." So indeed they are, in the final impression. They are, I should say, among the great characters in our fiction. They are memorable for their humanity, not merely their uniqueness or eccentricity; and in his great scenes they are memorable for their dignity, their capacity for feeling greatly. "If you doubt what I say," the telegram

[6] Mrs. Mabel Wheaton, who has kindly given me a copy.

concludes, "read over chapter on Ben's death and burial scenes that follow, then ask if anyone dares say these are not great people." One might dare after reading some other scenes; but I believe there is no question of Wolfe's sincerity, or of his actual accomplishment at his best.[7]

His best is in the chapter he mentions. Although Ben, his favorite brother, does not seem quite so tragic and grand a figure as Wolfe felt, his death evokes a scene worthy of high tragedy. It is a superb example of the "method of irony." For Wolfe here achieves grandeur, not by facile eloquence, not by ringing solemn bells, but by an utterly precise, terrible truthfulness, with a deliberate emphasis on incongruous detail.

Thus the scene takes place in Eliza's boarding house, a bleak, ugly monument of the blind acquisitiveness to which she has sacrificed the comfort and pride of the family. Old Gant, himself dying slowly of cancer, rocks petulantly, spits into the fire, moans. "To think that this should be put upon me, old and sick as I am. O Jesus, it's fearful—"

Eliza is busy with useless kettles of hot water, still hoping for the best, partly from habit, but chiefly in the grief and terror of the knowledge that her dying son does not wish to see her. Helen is hoarse and hysterical in her weariness and anguish: now furiously resentful of the behavior of her father and mother; now weeping in simple grief and pity; now comforting herself with the thought, announced with a "brooding ugly satisfaction," that she

[7] From conversations I have had with various people, I gather that almost all whom Wolfe put in his novels are now happy to be there. At any rate, only one libel suit grew out of the novel.

hasn't been to bed for two days and nobody can say she hasn't done everything she could. Even Eugene becomes human and credible in his habitual fury, horror and despair. "He felt that he might be clean and free if he could only escape into a single burning passion—hard, and hot, and glittering—of love, hatred, terror, or disgust. But he was caught, he was strangling, in the web of futility—there was no moment of hate that was not touched by a dozen shafts of pity." And his brother Luke, who occasionally responds to all the sham of life with a sudden roar of "idiot devastation," but more habitually lives in a world of large, gaudy symbols labeled "Family," "Honor," and "Generosity," is now painting all the conventional sentiments in crude capital letters:

"D-d-don't worry about his f-f-fighting," said Luke, in a rush of eulogy. "That b-b-boy'll fight as long as he's g-g-got a breath left in him."

"Why, yes," Eliza began, "I remember when he was a child of seven—I know I was standing on the porch one day—the reason I remember is Old Mr. Buckner had just come by with butter and eggs your papa had—"

"O my God!" groaned Helen, with a loose grin. "Now we'll get it."

"Whah—whah!" Luke chortled crazily, prodding Eliza in the ribs.

"I'll vow, boy!" said Eliza angrily. "You act like an idiot. I'd be ashamed!"

"Whah—whah—whah!"

Helen sniggered, nudging Eugene.

"Isn't he crazy, though? Tuh-tuh-tuh-tuh-tuh." Then, with wet eyes, she drew Eugene roughly into her big bony embrace.

"Poor old 'Gene. You always got on together, didn't you? You'll feel it more than any of us."

"He's not b-b-buried yet," Luke cried heartily. "That boy

51

may be here when the rest of us are pushing d-d-daisies."
"Where's Mrs. Pert?" said Eugene. "Is she in the house?"
A strained and bitter silence fell upon them.

Mrs. Pert, a former boarder of Eliza's, is a fat, warm,
hazy, alcoholic, middle-aged woman to whom the lonely
Ben had turned for comfort and love. Eliza had turned her
out. Now she repeats grimly: Mrs. Pert is a whore; Helen
indignantly defends the lady, as the only friend Ben ever
had; and again the loves and loyalties of the family end in
"the ugly clamor of their dissension."

But finally the family are summoned to the bleak room
where Ben lies, his gasping breath now a feeble rattle.
They grow quiet, they plunge below "the splintered
wreckage of their lives," they draw together "in a superb
communion of love and valiance, beyond horror and confusion, beyond death." The tobacco-stained doctor tells
them gently, with a "weary yellow smile," that nothing
more can be done; and picking up "his greasy black slouch
hat" he pronounces a tender benediction and departs. The
nurse—a distant poor relation—announces "with ugly and
triumphant matter-of-factness" that it will be a relief to get
it all over. Eliza now holds the hand of her unconscious
son, sitting very erect by his bed, "stiffly and primly like
a little child," her white face set stonily. Eugene realizes
with horror that her tight grip on Ben's hand is "an act of
union with her own flesh," that a part of her, the younger,
lovelier, long-forgotten part, was dying. She does not
loosen her grip until the last moment, when the rattling
in Ben's wasted body finally ceases.

But suddenly, marvellously, as if his resurrection and rebirth had
come upon him, Ben drew upon the air in a long and powerful

respiration; his gray eyes opened. Filled with a terrible vision of all life in the one moment, he seemed to rise forward bodilessly from his pillows without support—a flame, a light, a glory—joined at length in death to the dark spirit who had brooded upon each footstep of his lonely adventure on earth; and, casting the fierce sword of his glance with utter and final comprehension upon the room haunted with its gray pageantry of cheap loves and dull consciences and on all those uncertain mummers of waste and confusion fading now from the bright window of his eyes, he passed instantly, scornful and unafraid, as he had lived, into the shades of death.

No contemporary novelist, I believe, has more triumphantly resolved more complex disharmonies, or more powerfully struck the major chords of emotion.

The sequel is a grotesque medley of expressions of love and sorrow, outbursts of hysterical, ribald laughter, and the sordid business of funeral arrangements. But this letdown also illustrates the imaginative quality of Wolfe's realism. It points to the advantages of his impassioned, artless devotion to Life, which permitted him to deal freely with the whole range of experience. At times he wrote in the unvarnished naturalistic manner, mentioning the unmentionable in such detail that he has shocked old-fashioned readers, and may distress any reader simply on grounds of taste; Eugene's raptures in particular are likely to be a little embarrassing.[8] Because of this brutal frankness, however, Wolfe also felt free to grow lyrical, to celebrate ecstatically the best in man and nature; and if often he too consciously sought beauty—the beauty, as

[8] "Oh, Ann! . . . Oh, you lovely bitch. . . . You Boston bitch. . . . Oh, Ann, you sweet, dumb whore, if you only knew how much I love you—"

E. M. Forster has said, "at which a novelist should never aim, though he fails if he does not achieve it,"—often he did achieve it, through the fusion of his realism and his lyricism. And he also felt free to attempt pure fantasy, as in the concluding scene with the ghost of Ben. This too has a grotesque quality, suggestive of *Alice in Wonderland*:

> There was silence again, while Eugene sought timorously for words.
>
> "I hope," he began presently, with a small cracked laugh, "I hope, then, this doesn't mean that I'm crazy?"
>
> "Why not?" said Ben, with a swift flickering grin. "Of course you're crazy."
>
> "Then," said Eugene slowly, "I'm imagining all this?"
>
> "In heaven's name!" Ben cried irritably. "How should I know? Imagining all what?"
>
> "What I mean," said Eugene, "is, are we here talking together, or not?"
>
> "Don't ask me," said Ben. "How should I know?"
>
> With a strong rustle of marble and a cold sigh of weariness, the angel nearest Eugene moved her stone foot and lifted her arm to a higher balance. The slender lily stipe shook stiffly in her elegant cold fingers.
>
> "Did you see that?" Eugene cried excitedly.
>
> "Did I see what?" said Ben, annoyed.
>
> "Th-th-that angel there!" Eugene chattered, pointing with a trembling finger. "Did you see it move? It lifted its arm."
>
> "What of it?" Ben asked irritably. "It has a right to, hasn't it? . . ."

The conversation ends with Eugene's lyrical vision of his future. Ben's eyes burn terribly in darkness, with no answer; the day comes; and Eugene, alone in the Square, standing for the last time by the sculptured angels on Gant's porch, gazes on the distant soaring ranges.

3

Up to a point, *Of Time and the River* may be considered as of a piece with *Look Homeward, Angel*—another huge length sliced off the story that Wolfe apparently will go on writing forever. Since I have reached this point, I should pause to remark that he is indeed taking an unconscionably long time in growing up. *Of Time and the River* still reads like a first novel. Although published six years after *Look Homeward, Angel*, it is full of the same extravagances and is not a more finished technical performance; Wolfe appears to have learned little or nothing about his craft. Offhand, in fact, *Look Homeward, Angel* comes off better in a comparison. It remains the most unified of his novels, lyrically and dramatically, because it naturally falls into a simple pattern. It covers a natural stage in a man's life; it tells with whole-hearted intensity the story of growing pains, which to the youth are very complicated but to the grown man an old story.[9] By contrast, *Of Time and the River* is an arbitrary slice of a man's life, with practically no plot unity, no climax, no dramatic beginning, middle and end. It has more breadth and variety because Eugene Gant has got out into the great world; it also seems more formless and muddled because he is lost there, at the end appearing to be just about where he was at the beginning.

Perhaps the best index to the range and the limits of

[9] It should be added, however, that this simple pattern was not so apparent in Wolfe's original manuscript, which began with the Civil War and contained a great deal of family history. Maxwell Perkins, his editor, gave the novel its unity by persuading Wolfe to leave out the history.

THOMAS WOLFE

Wolfe's capacities at this stage is the creation of Francis
Starwick, the esthete who is Eugene's best friend at
Harvard and who turns out to be a homosexual. On the
whole, it is an impressive creation. It is the more notable
because, though drawn from life, this is a kind of life
utterly foreign to the world of *Look Homeward, Angel*
and to Wolfe's natural bent. But it was too foreign for him
wholly to command. He never convinces us that Starwick
was quite so rare and brilliant a spirit as he declares—"one
of the most extraordinary figures of his generation." His
admiration of Starwick seems rather provincial; the un-
couth country boy is envious of the polished gentleman-
artist. The country boy is also exasperated by him, however, and becomes tiresome in his mimicry of Starwick's
precious accents: "The thing is so *utterly* French . . .
really *quite* astonishing . . . *terribly* amusing . . . per-
fectly *grand*." In his impassioned moments, on the other
hand, Starwick is apt to talk like Wolfe: "My God! to come
into this world scarce half made up, to have the spirit of
the artist and to lack his hide, to feel the intolerable and
unspeakable beauty, mystery, loveliness, and terror of this
immortal land—this great America—and a skin too sensitive, a hide too delicate and rare . . . to declare its
cruelty, its horror, falseness, hunger, the warped and
twisted soul of its frustration." Here Wolfe romanticizes
the pathetic story of Starwick's inadequate talent, as if it
were the tragic ruin of genius, because he identifies himself with Starwick and conceives the frustration of the
artist as the most terrible of life's cruelties. The basic uncertainty of his conception is most apparent in the closing
scenes, where Starwick emerges as "his friend, his brother

56

—and his mortal enemy." Wolfe is characteristically attempting to create a symbolic, mythical figure, and by his characteristic method of incongruity; but the only apparent basis for the mortal enmity is that Starwick got the girl for whom Eugene had a fancy. In the scene of their final parting—goodbye, my one true friend, and goodbye, my mortal enemy, and "Oh, to feel so, suffer so, and live so!"—the myth collapses into banality.

Hence when Wolfe died, three years after the appearance of *Of Time and the River,* with his subsequent work not yet published, the more critical obituaries generally expressed the attitude that still persists. It was agreed that he had splendid talent, energy, ambition; but he had no art, no perspective, no humor, no philosophy, no social consciousness—in effect, no mind. He was compared to an automobile "with unlimited horsepower, a tiny steering wheel, and no brakes." Others dated the automobile. "Wolfe belonged to the high-pitched, unreal 1920's . . ." wrote Louis Kronenberger. "When he died, young as he was, he had lived too long. For the soberer life that came after the 20's, when the accent fell not on the individual but on society, was something Wolfe could not understand." Kronenberger added that he "never acquired, of course, any values—either intellectual or moral—that were worth consideration." John Peale Bishop, on the other hand, placed Wolfe in the disenchanted 'thirties. Appreciating his values as a mythmaker, Bishop linked him with Hart Crane, as the two most conspicuous failures in recent American literature. Both Crane and Wolfe sought their subject in the greatness of America, but both found that the America they longed to celebrate did not exist. "Both

57

were led at last, on proud romantic feet, to Brooklyn. And what they found there they abhorred." The depression in particular killed Wolfe's faith, Bishop thought. Hence Wolfe could find no meaning, no structure, for *Of Time and the River*.

Such verdicts were understandable enough at the time. Although they should have been more generally revised after the appearance of *You Can't Go Home Again*, I cite them here chiefly to emphasize the real limits of Wolfe's achievement up to this point. His central meaning was not clear; his critics were confused about his purposes and his values because he was himself confused. Yet *Of Time and the River* does give signs that he was really developing, coming out of confusion. The signs may escape notice because they involve the realization of a few elementary truths that will be no revelation to the reader. They may be apparent chiefly in rereading, in the light of Wolfe's final accomplishment. I may be overemphasizing them here simply because it is the critic's business to make out unity and continuity, to get things into shape. Nevertheless this is the critic's business; and Wolfe does not have to be pounded into shape. He was in fact acquiring both moral and intellectual values, entering on the "soberer life that came after the 20's."

The most obvious sign of this growth is an increasing strain of self-criticism. Although Wolfe is still far from mastering his follies, as man and as artist, at least he now recognizes them. In *Look Homeward, Angel* he is pleased by his romantic image, proud of such discoveries as his dislike for "whatever fits too snugly in a measure"; he is pleased to be Dr. Faustus, at whatever cost of mad hunger, fury and despair, because this is the divine madness of the Artist; and while he admits his human failings, the grievous fault is always in the world around him. Although his romanticism is not shallow—he notes that his quality as a romantic was not "to escape out of life, but into it"— his realism is also youthful. He wants Life, which is a glowing abstraction, necessarily different from all the life he knows; he wants the world, even though the world is his natural enemy. In *Of Time and the River*, however, he becomes aware that his mad hunger may be literally mad, and its futility no sign of divinity. At moments "the hopeless and unprofitable struggle of the Faustian life" become "horribly evident." It is unprofitable, as Starwick points out to Eugene, because it is unnecessary as well as hopeless:

> Do you think that you will really gain in wisdom if you read a million books? Do you think you will find out more about life if you know a million people rather than yourself? Do you think you will get more pleasure from a thousand women than from two or three—see more if you go to a hundred countries instead of six?

Eugene does think so, or for the most part continues to act as if he does; but at least Wolfe no longer does. If he may still rant about the futility of ranting, and his passion may grow madder because he is horrified by the thought that it is mad, he is getting more distance between Eugene and himself, viewing his story with more detachment. Furthermore, his maturer attitudes are coloring the substance and quality of his narrative, not merely punctuating it with reflective passages. An incidental example is the appearance of a quieter, cooler satire, approaching subtlety, as in the skilful portrait of Professor Hatcher.

("He was one of those rare people who really 'chuckle,' and although there was no doubting the spontaneity and naturalness of his chuckle, it is also probably true that Professor Hatcher somewhat fancied himself as a chuckler.") Similarly there appears a quieter kind of drama, as in Eugene's experience with the Coulson household in England: the crisp, competent, self-assured Coulsons who are lost in fog, failure and ruin, always friendly but unapproachable behind "the armor of their hard bright eyes"; while their boarders, who have also lost something precious and irrecoverable, nightly improvise negro jazz, fighting their emptiness with a "deliberate, formidable, and mad intensity of a calculated gaiety, a terrifying mimicry of mirth," as the storm-wind howls through the dark trees around them. In this episode Wolfe handles his typical incongruities with something like the melancholy, ironic detachment of Joseph Conrad; and his tone differs from Conrad's less in its higher pitch than in its more apparent tenderness.

This relative sobriety is most notable in Wolfe's treatment of his family, especially his father and mother. They have not changed, but they appear more admirable and more pitiable in *Of Time and the River* than in *Look Homeward, Angel;* Wolfe is no longer taking out on them his own bitterness. In the death of Gant—another of his unforgettable scenes—he does complete justice to their humanity. There is horror enough, or possibly even too much: the old stone-cutter, long a spectre except for his grotesquely powerful hands, suffers from enough cancer to kill a battalion of ordinary men. There is also a quality of tenderness and pity that has been rare in Wolfe. In the

last conversation between Gant and Eliza he makes
amends, yet without sacrificing truthfulness:

"Eliza,"—he said—and at the sound of that unaccustomed word,
a name he had spoken only twice in forty years—her white face
and her worn brown eyes turned toward him with the quick and
startled look of an animal—"Eliza," he said quietly, "you have had
a hard life with me, a hard time. I want to tell you that I'm sorry."

And before she could move from her white stillness of shocked
surprise, he lifted his great right hand and put it gently down
across her own. And for a moment she sat there bolt upright,
shaken, frozen, with a look of terror in her eyes, her heart drained
of blood, a pale smile trembling uncertainly and foolishly on her
lips. Then she tried to withdraw her hand with a clumsy movement, she began to stammer with an air of ludicrous embarrassment,
she bridled, saying—"Aw-w, now, Mr. Gant. Well, now, I reckon,"
—and suddenly these few simple words of regret and affection did
what all the violence, abuse, drunkenness and injury of forty years
had failed to do. She wrenched her hand free like a wounded
creature, her face was suddenly contorted by that grotesque and
pitiable grimace of sorrow that women have had in moments of
grief since the beginning of time, and digging her fist into her
closed eye quickly with the pathetic gesture of a child, she lowered
her head and wept bitterly:

"It was a hard time, Mr. Gant," she whispered, "a hard time,
sure enough. . . ."

But presently she is ashamed of her tears, and adds
hastily, "Not that I'm blamin' you, Mr. Gant . . . I
reckon we were both at fault . . . there was always something strange-like about you that I didn't understand."
Then, drying her eyes, she returns to her dauntless self,
sublime and ridiculous in her optimism: "Well, now, Mr.
Gant, that's all over." Now he must set his mind on getting
well. She winks at him briskly. Half our ills are imagination, she adds sententiously. But if he'll just make up his

mind to it, he'll get well. They both have years before them, perhaps the best years of their life; they can now profit by their mistakes. "That's just exactly what we'll do!" A few minutes later blood is pouring out of his mouth and nostrils; and Mr. Gant is dead.

The matrix of all these developments in *Of Time and the River* is Wolfe's growing realization of the deep bonds that united him with his fellowmen. With nature the child-giant from the mountains had been one, but in society he had been one apart; he was "called" but had no clearly recognized or generally respected calling; and he had prized his loneliness as a token that his spirit, like Shelley's, was "tameless and swift and proud." But now Wolfe is less proud. After a drunken escapade that lands him in jail, Eugene comes out feeling more than remorse. He is conscious "of a more earthly, common, and familiar union with the lives of other men than he had ever known." Wolfe tells us that Shelley is no longer his favorite poet: the sense of "proud and lonely inviolability" that he had treasured in Shelley has lost its magic.

This consciousness of community is again an elementary discovery, and in part a matter of mood. It has not yet got into Wolfe's habitual feeling—for a long time he had been at home with his feeling of homelessness. Yet his new consciousness was clear and deep enough to be of decisive importance in the myth that he was living as well as writing. It gave him a self-knowledge that his intense self-consciousness had denied him; for only through identification with others can one really know one's self, only through a full recognition of the typical and communal can one fully realize his individuality. Wolfe's romantic individualism had stamped him as a familiar type and impeded the growth of a real individuality, much as the popular worship of personality hinders people from becoming real persons. By the same token, Wolfe now came closer to the sources of myth; for at its broadest and deepest the typical is the mythical. And the realization of the living truth in such truisms is not, perhaps, so elementary a discovery after all. As Thomas Mann has said, the mythical represents an early, primitive stage in the life of humanity, but a late and mature one in the life of the individual.

In this view, *Look Homeward, Angel* is embryonic myth, or myth in the earliest stage of concrete story, the symbolical meaning of which may not be apparent to the author. Often it harks back to the animism of the earliest stories. Eugene, Wolfe writes, belonged "to an older and simpler race of men"; for him "the sun was a lordly lamp to light him on his grand adventuring." His whole world, indeed, was intensely animated. Everything about him was alive and meaningful, full of natural magic, full of human quality. So, too, with his author. Although Wolfe was an acute observer of the form or look of things, the essence or quality was usually a projection of his own feelings, and therefore preternaturally intense. Habitually he wrote in metaphor rather than simile—not, like modern poets, because he was deliberately aiming at condensation or ambiguity, but because he immediately saw and felt in this way. Likewise his chants, his exaggerations, his various modes of self-indulgence are also modes of symbolizing and ritualizing his experience. This whole way of apprehending life, which may seem unbecoming in a modern writer, is to a degree the way of all imaginative writers. In Wolfe, it was an extreme degree.

This is one reason why *Look Homeward, Angel* has impressed many readers as a highly original book, despite the familiarity of its basic theme. If Wolfe got at life through his senses and emotions rather than his brains, this may at least be a good way for a writer to begin; and he had the courage of his innocence and his yearning. He set himself against the main currents in modern prose, the tendencies to an unvarnished realism, to a cool sophistication, to an elaborate subtlety—to the various manners which at best represent a striving for honesty and precision, but which also reflect a fear of letting go or of ever being uncomplicated. Wolfe had no such fear. He seems like an original because he brought back something very old in his direct, unabashed, lyrical expression of his sensations and emotions. At his best he achieved a genuine eloquence, in which his rhythms communicate the ebb and flow of a valid emotion. It is a simple kind of poetry, often like the antiphonal verse of the Old Testament, and its power or charm is as difficult to explain in anything but simple terms. The limitations and the excesses of Wolfe's prose-poetry are much easier to point to. After reading *An American Tragedy* or *Studs Lonigan*, however, one may find them easier to forgive.

Yet *Look Homeward, Angel* remains a very personal legend of a very young man who is literally lost and seeking an actual home. Already Wolfe begins to say that he can't go home again, but by home he means simply Asheville. Even in these terms, to be sure, the legend has universal significance: countless young men have felt lost, homeless, hungry for life, love and fame—and have believed themselves unique. Nevertheless Wolfe was still thinking primarily in personal terms, as the old myth-makers did not. He also differed from them in that where they perceived chiefly likenesses or identities, he perceived incongruities and profound oppositions as well. So must we all today; only in these complex terms can the myth still be valid. In his egocentricity, however, Wolfe magnified the oppositions, or even created them. And it is these that begin to dissolve in *Of Time and the River*. Although Wolfe is still confined to his own experience, incapable of a detached, objective view of the world around him, he now recognizes that his experience is not singular and that he has much in common with the world. Although he is prone to create other men in his own lonely image, he recognizes their community in loneliness, and despite loneliness. In general, his personal legend becomes increasingly typical and symbolical. Specifically, it becomes an American legend.

Thus his highly individualized, even eccentric characters are now presented as characteristic American products or types. His father's life is an American tragedy: the life of "the lost American who has been brought forth naked under immense and lonely skies, to 'shift for himself,' to grope his way blindly through the confusion and brutal chaos of a life as naked and unsure as he, to wander blindly down across the continent, to hunt forever for a goal, a wall, a dwelling place of warmth and certitude, a light, a door." In particular, old Gant is a symbol of the old pioneer America which has been increasingly corrupted by commercialism: thus as a young man he had carved a marble angel, in his dream of becoming a sculptor, and as an old man he sold it to ornament the grave of a whore. American, too, is the "dissonance and frenzied unrest" of Eugene's brother Luke, hurling himself along lonely roads at night, "going furiously from nowhere into nowhere, rushing ahead with starlight shining on his knit brows and his drawn face, with nothing but the lonely, mournful, and desolate red-clay earth about him, the immense, the merciless emptiness and calm of the imperturbable skies above him." Even the rare, the precious Francis Starwick turns out to be the son of a Mid-Western small-town school superintendent; and his story is at bottom the pitifully common one of a precious devotion to "culture" because of the "rawness" and "crudeness" of American life. So a host of unrelated characters, who had entered Wolfe's novel chiefly because they had entered his life, are now related to a common theme—the magnificent promise and the appalling blight of American life.

Similarly a host of sensuous images of the physical background become related to a more philosophical image. Initially, they owed much more to memory than to reflection; they constituted a panorama of America rather than a vision; and the meaning of the spectacle changed with Eugene's mood. Often Wolfe's image of America is an enchanted one of an immense, exultant, fabulous country "where miracles not only happen, but where they happen all the time." As often it is a disenchanted view of an immense desolation, ugliness, cruelty, savagery; the miracles do not happen. But now he is more earnestly seeking a central meaning, and more clearly perceiving that he must find it in precisely these violent contradictions. Eugene

66

makes the "desperate and soul-sickening discovery" that he must find goodness, truth and beauty, not in radiant, magical images, but in "the mean hearts of common men," in "all the blind and brutal complications" of the destiny of America. There, in ways still darklier and stranger than he had thought, lay his heart's desire: "buried there in the grimy and illimitable jungles of its savage cities—a-prowl and raging in the desert and half-mad with hunger in the barren land, befouled and smutted with the rust and grime of its vast works and factories, warped and scarred and twisted, stunned, bewildered by the huge multitude of all its errors and blind gropings, yet still fierce with life, still savage with its hunger, still broken, slain and devoured by its terrific earth, its savage wilderness—and still, somehow, God knows how, the thing of which he was a part, that beat in every atom of his blood and brain and life, and was indestructible and everlasting, and that was America!"

This whole development, finally, gives *Of Time and the River* a kind of form, which helps to explain the cumulative power of the novel that many readers feel even while they feel troubled by the absence of conventional plot or dramatic unity. As Joseph Warren Beach remarks, it is a musical form, comparable to a tone poem of Richard Strauss or a Wagnerian opera—or in the novel to Gide's *The Counterfeiters*. The central theme is the idea of a pilgrimage; the *leitmotifs* are the recurrent images of loneliness and hunger, the quest of a father, of a gate or door, of a tongue or word by which to articulate and "possess" all life; and the basic incongruities may serve as counterpoint. In terms of episode, the related themes are the pilgrimages of the Southerner to the North, of the country boy to the

67

big city, of the American to Europe—all projected against the background of time and the river, the pilgrimage of man's life on the timeless earth. Such elements of form are clearer when *Of Time and the River* is viewed in relation to Wolfe's whole "book," and in any view are blurred by considerable extraneous material. Unlike Gide, Wolfe did not consciously plan his novel so. Yet his central theme, at least, is clear and explicit; and as the passionate pilgrim becomes more conscious of its implications, the related themes emerge more clearly from the sprawl and dissonance of his experience.

The least significant of these themes is Wolfe's flight from the "lost and lonely South." He was indeed a self-conscious rebel, who wrote bitterly of the sterile romanticism of the South with its "swarming superstition," its "cheap mythology," its "hostile and murderous intrenchment against all new life." He accordingly angered many Southerners; one critic suggested that perhaps he "should be obliged, in the vast area of his sympathies, to make room for the people who bred him." In fact, however, Wolfe never lost his sympathy for these people. He always wrote with deep feeling of "Old Catawba," and its obscure but magnificent history "full of heroism, endurance, and the immortal silence of the earth"; in his last work he was writing this history. His very pride in it intensified his scorn of the legends of an "aristocratic culture," especially in South Carolina. At any rate, he had not been deeply affected by the romantic mythology of the South, and quickly outgrew his boyish attachment to it. For him the road to the "proud fierce North," the land of his father, was doubtless the road to freedom and life; his flight was a sign of the realistic quality of his own romanticism. Yet the North was not itself the land of freedom; he was no less critical of it, and lost and lonely in it. And though his criticism sometimes betrays the proud Southerner, who is sometimes embarrassed by a feeling of apostasy, this was a more or less incidental complication of his thought and feeling. The chief point is that no merely regional tradition could satisfy his hunger or provide an image large enough for his belief and his power.

Hence the most significant experience that the North afforded Wolfe was the experience of cosmopolitan New York, the melting pot of rural as well as foreign-born America, and the symbol of the multitudinous life he had a passion to absorb. This stage of his pilgrimage reveals his exceptional ability to recapture the marvelous and the mythical in the commonplace. Because the coming of a country boy to the big city is so old a tale, we are apt to forget what a thrilling, magical and meaningful adventure it is; and no other writer has rendered its quality so fully and so glowingly as has Wolfe. But this experience is also fundamental to his whole legend. Inevitably he was disillusioned by New York, unable to digest its multitudes, and his revulsion inspired his blackest, bitterest pages. Necessarily he had to outgrow or transcend this disillusionment if his myth was to accommodate the terms of modern experience. For if New York is not the whole of America, it is the symbol of modern industrial America at its best and its worst. It is the quintessential manifestation of the exuberant energy and the might of a polyglot land; of the fabulous power of "natural knowledge" expressed in the soar of skyscrapers, the sweep of bridges, the blaze

69

of swarming streets; of the grandeur and the glory realized in concrete, steel and glass. It is also the quintessence of the grime and filth, the dreary waste, the raucous vulgarity, the blatant materialism, the brutal violence of industrial America. So must it be accepted, as magnificent monument and as foul blot. So Wolfe did in time accept it. "And that was America!" was the conclusion of his "desperate and soul-sickening discovery." If the discovery seems needlessly desperate, at least he earned his exclamation point.

The turning point in his experience, however, was the pilgrimage to Europe. In Europe he saw a way of life magical in its grace, its form, its assurance; here were people who had found a way, a door; here were actual pleasure and joy, immediately realized and shared, instead of the lonely joys of expectancy and promise that he knew in America. Yet it was an alien life, he could not enter this door or share this joy; he remained a lonely American who could thrill only to the splendid promise. As he wandered, his memories and his desires were extraordinarily intensified by his aching homelessness. And so he discovered America, he tells us, by leaving it. His years abroad made him realize his profound need of it.

This discovery no doubt owed something to the jealous pride of the provincial, and a resentment of the European condescension toward America. But Wolfe was also a sensitive, penetrating observer. While fully appreciating both the superficial charms and the deep satisfactions of the ancient culture of Europe, he saw clearly the vanities, the ancient fears and hatreds, the corruption and decay be-

70

neath the charming surface.[10] He thereby got a perspective on the notorious limitations of America. If Americans were provincial and cocky, the British were no less insular and complacent; if they were materialistic, they had no more reverence for the dollar than French peasants and merchants had for the sou; if they were standardized, the very superiority of Europe was supposed to lie in its settled manners or standardized way of life. Although Wolfe did not formulate the generalization, in effect he began to realize that every society must have the defects of its virtues, its over-emphases and under-emphases. The glory of Europe lies in its traditional way of life; but tradition preserves a great deal of junk as well as precious achievement, and a reverence for it can also be a symptom of stagnation. The limitations of America lie in its raw, reckless youth; but youth is also the source of its energy, vitality, humor, faith and hope.

Hence Wolfe was able to end *Of Time and the River* on a triumphant note that does not sound forced or shrill. The wanderer returns from Europe, more enthralled by the homecoming than was Ulysses. Wolfe describes the voyage to America as "the supreme ecstasy of the modern world." "There is no other experience that is remotely comparable to it, in its sense of joy, its exultancy, its drunken

[10] Wolfe was especially critical of the French, and as early as 1925 his letters to his mother predict their downfall before the Germans. His comments on the British are also suggestive: "We are taught in America to dislike the English, and to believe in the French. It is simple madness. The English are often insolent, and frequently jealous of our commercial power, but they have character and I believe, down below all the rest, a certain feeling of kinship with us. Moreover, they have a fundamental honesty."

and magnificent hope which, against reason and knowledge, soars into a heaven of fabulous conviction, which believes in the miracle and sees it invariably achieved." Here Wolfe is mythicizing, in the heroic manner; and good Americans may be embarrassed. Yet if this grandiloquence is "against reason and knowledge," Wolfe by now does have the reason and knowledge. His view of America is far more realistic, complex and ironic than was, say, Homer's view of Greece. He has not come by his enthrallment easily or cheaply; and once we have modestly admitted that a trip to America is not the supreme ecstasy, we may be grateful for the ecstasy that he has legitimately recaptured. His primary gift as a mythmaker, once more, was this quick feeling for the wonderful strangeness of the familiar, the enchantments of routine modern experience.

Meanwhile Wolfe's growing awareness of the meaning of his legend has not yet brought the peace, strength and wisdom he is seeking. His image of America is very large, and none too clear or steady; his supreme ecstasy at the end of *Of Time and the River* is not a supreme certainty. Moreover, Wolfe's emotion will swell to fit this mighty subject, and swell the more because his America too is created in his own image. In his exultant moods he must now celebrate not only his own youthful hopes but the power and promise of a youthful nation; in his dark, bitter moods he must now agonize over not only his personal frustrations but the loneliness and waste of American life. He still has too few general ideas, and too little interest in such ideas. He has the more need of them because he still has a great deal of unemployed emotion.

Yet the important thing is that Wolfe is finding a meaning for his book. It will become more explicit, it will broaden and deepen; but the design is already apparent. Granted that all Wolfe's discoveries are rather elementary, as well as rather belated, the really effective ideas in human history—the great ideas by which men and nations live—are usually platitudes. His discoveries are at least an adequate groundwork for his myth—myths do not require novel or highly original themes. And so with a still more elementary and more fundamental discovery that is stressed in the closing pages of *Of Time and the River*. In the little towns of France an ancient faith, latent in Wolfe's blood, was quietly but powerfully awakened. His senses, his heart, his mind were filled with rich, drowsy sensations of the unutterable familiarity of this strange world. Life in these towns, he was pleased to rediscover, was the same as life in the little towns of America, and everywhere on earth. "And after all the dark and alien world of night, of Paris, and another continent . . . this re-discovery of the buried life, the fundamental structure of the great family of earth to which all men belong, filled him with a quiet certitude and joy."

More specifically, the sound of a cathedral bell, as Wolfe sat in a cobbled square in the ancient city of Dijon, served him much like the famous *madeleine* that inspired Proust's *Remembrance of Things Past*. With the sound of the old bell, "everything around him burst into instant life," a life he had always known. His school bell, the distant chimes on a street at night, the lonely sounds of old Catawba—a host of long-forgotten things swarmed back, incredibly alive and near. Then, after a moment of brooding silence, began the sound of men going home for lunch; and Wolfe was closer to the lost America of his childhood than he would ever be when in America:

They came with solid, lonely, liquid shuffle of their decent leather, going home, the merchants, workers, and good citizens of that old town of Dijon. They streamed across the cobbles of that little square; they passed, and vanished, and were gone forever— leaving silence, the brooding hush and apathy of noon, a suddenly living and intolerable memory, instant and familiar as all this life around him, of a life that he had lost, and that could never die.

It was the life of twenty years ago in the quiet, leafy streets and little towns of lost America—of an America that had been lost beneath the savage roar of its machinery, the brutal stupefaction of its days, the huge disease of its furious, ever-quickening and incurable unrest. . . . And now, all that lost magic had come to life again here in the little whitened square, here in this old French town, and he was closer to his childhood and his father's life of power and magnificence than he could ever be again in savage new America; and as the knowledge of these strange, these lost yet familiar things returned to him, his heart was filled with all the mystery of time, dark time, the mystery of strange million-visaged time that haunts us with the briefness of our days.

This experience obviously helped Wolfe to amplify the meaning of his legend, by linking the pilgrimage of a lost American with the universal destiny of lonely man. So he had felt at the death of old Gant, that his father was unlike any other man who had ever lived, and that every man who ever lived was like his father. Less obviously, however, this experience also threatened to cut short his pilgrimage or narrow its meaning. Like Proust, Wolfe was seeking to recapture his whole past experience, through his sensory impressions; but like Proust he sometimes sought the remembrance of things past as a refuge, an escape from adult frustrations. He hankered to go home again, to this lost America, the world of his childhood; his quest of a father sometimes looks more like the quest of a mother, a yearning for the womb—we may recall that he was not weaned until he was three and a half years old. Yet Wolfe did not go home again, finally. He returned instead to the actual America. Literally and figuratively, he returned to his senses: the exceptionally alert, acute senses that were the springs of his art. And the abiding value of his experience in the ancient towns of France, even if he did not clearly realize it, was that it deepened and clarified this source of his strength.

Unlike Proust, Wolfe did not attempt a minute analysis of all his sensory impressions, or an elaborate rationalization of his whole method; he did not erect his intuitive practice into a Bergsonian philosophy of intuitionism. The most difficult problem that he wrestled with, he explains in *The Story of a Novel*, was the problem of time; but his concept of time was a very simple one, not mystical or metaphysical. He wanted to give at once the sense of the actual present in its continuous flow, the sense of past time as living in the present and at every moment conditioning the lives of his characters, and the sense of time immutable —the timeless time of earth and sea against which would be projected the transience of man's life. He wanted, in other words, to render permanence and change as they are felt in immediate experience, in which both are very real; whereas Proust, like the mystics, aspired to the realm of pure Time, the realm of Essence or Being, where change is mere appearance. And the sensory image, fully apprehended, was the key to Wolfe's time problem, the means of rendering at once the transient and the timeless. It is the

75

carrier of the essential meanings of art, the key to its magical union of the material and the ideal, the passing and the surpassing; for the universal and the eternal are realized only in the particular, and our loftiest, rarest, most "spiritual" ideas are stirred by sensory images, brought home by them, and embodied in them. Through the senses, so commonly despised by philosophers, by theologians, by scientists and even by poets in their Platonic moods, one is led to an intense realization of natural continuities, the rhythms of the universe, the vast enveloping whole; and so one may apprehend the "deeper reality" or "higher reality" that all aspire to.

In short, Wolfe was now realizing more than the face value of his extraordinarily keen senses and retentive memory, which make possible the uncommon perceptions, the deep associations and the complex syntheses that are one way of defining genius.

3. THE STORY OF A NOVEL

IN 1935, THE YEAR WHEN *OF TIME AND THE RIVER* APPEARED, Wolfe also published two other books, *From Death to Morning* and *The Story of a Novel.*[1] The former is a collection of short pieces which, with a few exceptions, add little to his stature or to our understanding of him. Mostly they are not complete, self-contained short stories but sketches, little pieces of novel. They are in fact pieces that he was unable to fit into his novels, or forced to edit out, and are worth salvaging chiefly because they have the same substance and quality as the novels. In addition there are a few exercises from a writer's notebook: "Only the Dead Know Brooklyn," a tiresome exercise in Brooklynese; "One of the Girls in Our Party," an experiment in the Ring Lardner manner, but less amusing and more obvious than Lardner; "The Far and the Near," a bare outline for a

[1] *The Story of a Novel* was published in book form in 1936, but it first appeared as a series of articles in the *Saturday Review of Literature* in December, 1935.

potentially good short story. On the whole, the collection emphasizes that Wolfe needed plenty of room, and was seldom capable of the artistry required by the confinement of the short story. A little Wolfe is not apt to go a long way.

The best thing in this volume, accordingly, is a novelette, "The Web of Earth." It is a monologue by Eliza, who talks to her son and is allowed to tell her own story, without benefit of comment or chant by the author. It is perhaps Wolfe's most expert technical performance, for he achieves form through the method of apparent formlessness. Eliza talks out of her inexhaustible memory; one thing leads to another, by psychological rather than logical association; but by the end she has woven the complete pattern of a personality and a life, against the background of the good earth. There is also some of Wolfe's best writing in an overlong sketch called "Death the Proud Brother." His account, for example, of a nondescript little Irishman who died in a New York subway station is precise, sensitive and eloquent despite its typical overload of adjective and epithet:

Poor, shabby, servile, fawning, snarling, and corrupted cipher, poor, meager, cringing, contriving, cunning, drearily hopeful, and dutifully subservient little atom of the million-footed city. Poor, dismal, ugly, sterile, shabby little man—with your little scrabble of harsh oaths, and cries, and stale constricted words, your pitiful little designs and feeble purposes, with your ounce of brain, your thimbleful of courage, the huge cargo of your dull and ugly superstitions. Oh, you wretched little thing of dough and tallow, you eater of poor foods and drinker of vile liquors. Joy, glory, and magnificence were here for you upon this earth, but you scrabbled along the pavements rattling a few stale words like gravel in your throat, and would have none of them, because the smell of the boss, the word of the priest, the little spare approvals of Mike, Mary,

Molly, Kate, and Pat were not upon them—and tonight the stars shine, great ships are blowing from the harbor's mouth, and a million more of your own proper kind and quality go stamping on above your head, while you sit here *dead* in your gray tunnel!

Another revealing piece, though intrinsically unimportant, is "Gulliver," a wry essay in which Wolfe tells how his tallness always set him apart from his fellows. "The great distances of this world are the fractional ones," he remarks, and he writes convincingly of all the unvarying questions and stale jests he had had to endure. He concludes, less convincingly, that from this experience he had learned not only a stern humanity but a faith in the essential goodness of man. It is evident that an important source of his youthful bitterness was this incongruity in himself, that so fine a spirit should be lodged in so monstrous a carcass.

Far more significant, however, is *The Story of a Novel*. With the generally favorable, even enthusiastic reception of *Of Time and the River*, Wolfe felt assured of his position as a writer. Despite his apparent egotism, he had needed such assurance; he had been oppressed by the responsibilities of his fame as a "young American writer," tortured by the fear that he might be a flash in the pan, another one-book writer. Now he paused to take stock. In *The Story of a Novel* he reviews his accomplishment and outlines the task ahead. It is an unassuming, utterly truthful little book. No writer, not even Trollope, has written about his own work with more quiet, unaffected honesty; an honesty the more difficult because Wolfe's work had been conceived and wrought with such passion. He is not only humble but free from false modesty, and not only earnest but clear-sighted; he gives a very just statement of his methods and aims, his failures and successes. In particular, he clearly defines and explains the mature attitudes that in *Of Time and the River* might be overlooked, or discounted as passing moods, because they do not clearly govern the conception of the work as a whole. His story of his novel makes it much plainer that he has grown considerably.

It is no detraction from Wolfe's sincerity and truthfulness to add at once that he will continue to commit the sins that he here confesses to, and will not fulfill the promise of this sober story. For he himself qualifies the promise. He emphasizes that he is never able to learn easily or surely, by taking counsel or studying example, but has to learn everything by himself through endless trial and error, with endless confusion, waste and torment. "I am not a professional writer," he admits at the outset. "I am not even a skilled writer . . . I don't know how to write a novel yet." He goes on to specify his faults: his addiction to adjectives, to chants and catalogues, to "Amount and Number," to overabundance and overexplicitness. He recognizes "a quality of intemperate excess" in his whole effort "to include more, experience more, than the measure of one life can hold, or than the limits of a single work of art can well define." He perceives that what critical faculties he had were seriously impaired by his frenzied labors. He tells wryly of how he had written a 100,000-word novel merely as an introductory chapter to *Of Time and the River*, how he battled with his editor against cutting, and how when he did cut, his "soul recoiled before the carnage of so many lovely things."

This novel, Wolfe makes clear, was conceived in a somewhat different spirit from *Look Homeward, Angel*, or in a sense was not conceived at all. Although it seems like a simple continuation of the early novel, the second installment of his autobiography, this obvious plan apparently had not occurred to Wolfe. For some months he kept writing notes and fragments, without aim, with increasing torment. He went to Paris, in search of "a place to work," but found only a desperate homesickness. His passion swelled, he was racked by a "constant and almost intolerable effort of memory and desire." Then, suddenly, the dam burst; and his book came in a torrential flood that swept him along for more than four years. He "cannot really say the book was written"; rather, it was something that took hold of him, "possessed" him, and almost did for him. He might have quoted Henry James: "You must be *possessed*, and you must strive to possess your possession." Wolfe never did possess his completely, and at that he needed outside help; his editor had to convince him that his book was finished. He summarizes its composition as "a progress that began in a whirling vortex and a creative chaos and that proceeded slowly at the expense of infinite confusion, toil, and error toward clarification and the articulation of an ordered and formal structure." His editor helped him to make out this structure, and to lay it bare by cutting out huge layers of fat.

Manifestly this is not the best way to write novels. All that Wolfe can say is that it was the only possible way for him; the demon within him could not be reasoned out of him, but had to be lived out. At the same time, Wolfe is not merely humble and apologetic. He remarks as quietly his possession of unusual sensory and creative powers. Although he now realizes that what matters is the depth and intensity, not the extent of experience, he is also wise enough not simply to regret his insane hunger and his frenzied labors. Despite all the waste and torment they cost, he believes that the "total quality" of the whole experience was "not useless or excessive." It finally brought him closer to a true estimate of his talents, a concrete definition of his resources, a living apprehension of the substance, the language and the conscience he needs as man and as artist. Now he believes with all his heart that he has found the right way, the door he sought. Nevertheless he does not promise a complete reform: he is just beginning to find himself, "the door is not yet open." As for craftsmanship, he agrees with his editor that he will never be a perfectionist, a Flaubert.

This is something of an understatement. Wolfe also understates his autobiographical tendency when he confesses that he "may have written" *Look Homeward, Angel* "with a certain naked intensity of spirit which is likely to characterize the earliest work of a young writer." At any rate, *The Story of a Novel* disposes of any possible question about how directly and spontaneously he wrote out of his own experience, in his own way, without conscious plan or specific artistic purpose. Hence he stood outside the literary movements of his time, even when they were moving in the same direction as he. Any resemblance between Wolfe's characters and living persons is never accidental; any resemblance between Wolfe and other writers is largely incidental. This is most plain when we look at the most conspicuous literary influence on his work, which he acknowledges here—the influence of James Joyce.

On occasion Wolfe used the technique of the "Wandering Rocks" episode in *Ulysses*—a series of disconnected scenes about unrelated characters, or related only in their contemporaneity; as Joyce presented a cross-section of Dublin in this way, so Wolfe presents Asheville in the early morning.[2] He also liked Joyce's device of alternating sharply contrasted styles for mock-heroic or mock-poetic purposes:

> At this moment, with a smooth friction of trotting rumps, the death-wagon of Rogers-Malone turned swiftly in from the avenue, and wheeled by on ringing hoofs. They turned curiously and watched it draw up to the curb.
> "Another Redskin bit the dust," said George Graves.
> Come, delicate death, serenely arriving, arriving.
> "Horse" Hines came out quickly on long flapping legs, and opened the doors behind.

Wolfe picked up some other stylistic mannerisms, such as the trick of compounding words, inverting, piling up sensuous adjectives:

> Smiling with imperturbable tenderness, Mrs. Selborne thrust out her heavy legs slowly to swell with warm ripe smack his gift of flowered green-silk garters. Wetting his thumb with sly thin after-smile, he told.

Still another exercise in Joycean poetry is this:

> Far-forested, a horn-note wound. Sea-forested, water-far, the grotted coral sea-far horn-note. The pillioned ladies witch-faced in bottle-green robes saddle-swinging. Merwomen unscaled and lovely in sea-floor colonnades. The hidden land below the rock. The flitting wood-girls growing into bark. Far-faint, as he wakened, they besought him with lessening whir.

And the whole chapter of the train ride in *Of Time and the River* is full of tricks learned from Joyce.

[2] Chapter 14, *Look Homeward, Angel.*

Yet all these are but five-finger exercises, flights of fancy that when most successful are still only flights, exhibiting Wolfe's gift of mimicry but not his essential manner. In theory, Joyce might have been an excellent influence, teaching him much about his craft, especially how to maintain distance from his materials; or he might have been a ruinous influence, teaching the young writer meanings and methods alien to his own talent and experience. In fact, Joyce exercised only a superficial influence. Wolfe did not learn from him a significantly new way of looking at things or writing about them.

Thus an important symbol that they both use—the search for a father—has a far simpler meaning for Wolfe and leads to nothing like the elaborate symbolism of *Ulysses*.[3] And here we may be pleased that Wolfe went his own way. For Joyce, the father-son motif is only one of the many themes artfully woven into the amazingly intricate pattern of *Ulysses*, and does not seem like the animating principle of the book; the uninitiated reader might miss entirely the supposed significance of the final meeting of father-Bloom and son-Dedalus, for neither seems much affected by their meeting. For Wolfe, however, this symbol is much more than a literary device. The father is a natural symbol of the strength and wisdom he sought, and could not find in his actual father, who was also lost. He treated the symbol with something like the complete seriousness

[3] Apparently Wolfe got this idea of the search for a father from Maxwell Perkins rather than Joyce. Perkins declares that he suggested it casually as a literal subject for a picaresque novel, and was surprised when Wolfe picked it up eagerly for his own purposes. Then he too realized that it symbolized a meaning which was already at the heart of Wolfe's work.

and artless sincerity—call it freshness, call it naïveté—of the old mythmakers.

For the rest, Wolfe indeed read voluminously and voraciously, if not quite a million books, and his reading fed his passion to be a great writer, swelled his rhetoric. But he got from it essentially what all readers get, especially young ones. It helped to form and fill his mind; it did not directly shape his art. His taste is notable chiefly for its catholicity. In his novels he tells how he enjoyed the Elizabethans and the Victorians, the Augustans and the Romantics; he expresses his admiration at once for Scott, Dickens, Dostoyevsky, Melville, Hardy, and Joyce; he is particularly enthusiastic about the "great fabulists," but these include such diverse figures as Homer, Shakespeare, Voltaire, Euripides, Swift, Coleridge, Aristophanes and Poe; and he is equally enthusiastic about their irony and their passion. The few masters he could not enjoy were apparently those whose art was more exquisite than robust; he mentions that he was unable to finish a single novel by James or Howells.

Perhaps it is ordinarily better for young writers to show more partiality in their reading, to reject more; they may then strengthen their own individuality as writers, follow more surely their natural bent. But Wolfe's catholicity was natural to him, in keeping with his essential soundness as well as his simplicity. "Nearly everything in the world of books that has touched my life most deeply," he wrote, "has come from authority." Although he wrote directly out of his own experience, he wrote with all literature behind him, and in him. "The historical sense," T. S. Eliot has said, "involves a perception not only of the pastness of the past, but of its presence; the historical sense compels a man to write not merely with his own generation in his bones, but with a feeling that the whole of the literature of Europe from Homer and within it the whole of the literature of his own country has a simultaneous existence and composes a simultaneous order. This historical sense . . . is what makes a writer traditional." By this definition, Wolfe was a more traditional writer than most even of his conservative, pious contemporaries—or than Eliot himself. At least his catholicity helped him to find himself while his more fastidious contemporaries were looking down on the Victorians or the Romantics, or discrediting the bulk of our literary heritage as bourgeois.

Thus Wolfe quickly saw through the vanities of Professor Hatcher's "advanced" students and the literary salons of Boston, with their self-conscious modernity, their bored condescension toward the greater writers of the immediate past, their terribly insistent cleverness and knowingness, their glib jargon of the arts, their calculated pleasure in "what was called 'the exchange of ideas,' but what most often was merely the exchange of other people's ideas." If this higher artiness now seems obviously silly, it nevertheless took in even serious, talented writers—and in its subtler forms still does. Wolfe's impassioned belief that the life of the artist is "the best, the rarest, and the highest" on earth may be called romantic, yet he always knew that this life can be won "only by bitter toil and knowledge and stern living." Again, like many others who were "looking for a place to write," Wolfe went to Europe, but he soon discovered that the place to write was Hammersmith, Brooklyn, Keokuk, or any place on earth, so long as he had the faith, the power, and the passion within him; whereas others continued to flee to Paris or to New York, and then away from New York back to the hometown, or to little colonies in New England or New Mexico. He soon shook off as well "the fancied woes and hardships of the young artist in conflict with the dull and brutal philistines," the fashionable myth that no really sensitive, imaginative boy could make good in this crass society of ours. Even while Wolfe was still admiring H. L. Mencken as the contemporary critic of "the greatest range and power," and was at times still feeling very daring and emancipated as he scorned all the boobs and Baptists, he was ranging far beyond Mencken and by himself discovering far deeper sources of power.

By himself and in the hard way—this must be repeated, not to celebrate Wolfe's honesty or to patronize his naïveté, but simply to know him. No doubt he learned something from Dreiser, Anderson, Lewis and other American realists. No doubt he was also fortunate in that he did not learn some of the current lessons in beauty and truth. The fact remains, for better and for worse, that he was essentially an untaught artist, a self-made man. Even his up-to-date realism is a product of his teeming memory, an inheritance from his mother, and is undirected, as unconfined, by literary doctrine. It is at times naturalistic, at times symbolistic; but the naturalism springs chiefly from his personal revulsion against his immediate environment, the symbolism from his blazing dream and desire. Similarly his literary development centers primarily in his growth as a man rather than as a craftsman, in the solution of his philosophical rather than his technical problems. The most important revelation of *The Story of a Novel*, therefore, is of the progress he has made in his search for a father, a door, a home.

Wolfe here tells at considerable length how his stay in Europe intensified his senses, his memories and his desires, and thereby led to his discovery of America. But he also dwells on the deepest and most salutary influence on his later career, which is not made explicit in *Of Time and the River*. This was the great depression of the 'thirties, which he experienced in Brooklyn. Contrary to John Peale Bishop's belief, it did not destroy his faith in America—it was indeed the means to his faith.[4] Wolfe's image of America had been primarily a literary, sensuous image of the physical features, rhythms, manners, folkways. Although it was not sentimental or merely picturesque, it was not a philosophical image; it symbolized a kind of strength but not the wisdom that Wolfe needed. More specifically, he had not penetrated to the economic realities behind both the splendid and the ugly appearances, to the foundations of the common life, the "common family of earth" from which he had sprung and against which he had rebelled. Now he tells how he lived in Brooklyn for three years, during the depths of the depression. As he struggled with his giant work, unable to sleep, he nightly prowled through the jungle of the city; and so he "saw, lived, felt,

[4] Hart Crane, on the other hand, was defeated by Brooklyn. In "The Bridge" he attempted a "mystical synthesis of America," but he failed because he at length could not really believe in his epical theme. He was oppressed by the idea that to his fellowmen the mighty symbol of the Bridge meant only "an economical approach to shorter hours, quicker lunches, behaviorism and toothpicks."

and experienced the full weight of that horrible human calamity."

The immediate impact of this experience was the more staggering because it was a black time in Wolfe's own life. He declares that he would never lose the conviction he got from it, "of man's inhumanity to his fellow man, the unending repercussions of those scenes of suffering, violence, oppression, hunger, cold, and filth and poverty going on unheeded in a world in which the rich were still rotten with their wealth." Yet he also writes that never in his life had he lived so fully, "shared so richly in the common life of man"; his senses, his powers of feeling, reflection and memory, reached "the greatest degree of sharpness" that they had ever known. And he is now grateful for this black period. It left "a burning memory . . . of the fortitude of man, his ability to suffer and somehow to survive" —and of his own ability to share these qualities. It added to his stature as man and as artist.

This heightening, broadening and deepening of Wolfe's social consciousness did not culminate in a complete social philosophy or a political program. To his embattled contemporaries, indeed, he still seemed lacking in social consciousness. Wolfe felt obliged to defend his conviction that his own job was to write novels, not tracts, and that he could not do this job well if he took time off to accept all the invitations to convocations or cocktail parties for the benefit of the Spanish Republicans and other worthy causes. In an interview, he was at pains to remark that his own people were all working people; but his main argument was that an artist's life depends upon a knowledge

of all people. "As you go on, what you write becomes less
concerned with Bill as a person to justify yourself and
you're able to enlarge upon experience so that Bill's or
Tom's experience becomes interesting and significant to
you only in terms of its relation to general humanity . . .
and if that's not social consciousness, I don't know what
the hell it is." At any rate, he in fact did have a new
consciousness, and a more sober conscience, which went
deeper than the new political fervor of some of his fellow
writers. It made a lasting difference in his thinking and
feeling.

In *Look Homeward, Angel* there is scarcely a trace of
such interests. Wolfe explicitly disavows any political
interest: Eugene "was quite content with any system
which might give him comfort, security, enough money
to do as he liked, and freedom to think, eat, drink, love,
read, and write what he chose. And he did not care under
what form of government he lived—Republican, Demo-
crat, Tory, Socialist, or Bolshevist—if it could assure him
these things. He did not want to reform the world. . . ."
Political interests are not required of artists, to be sure;
but the young Wolfe apparently regarded them as an in-
significant manifestation of Life, or even unbecoming the
Artist. Such casual reflections as he does indulge in his
youthful letters to his mother are chiefly vulgar prejudices,
or smart ideas picked up from Mencken. He worries over
the hordes of Jews, Italians, Greeks and other "inferior
people" who threaten to ruin America; he parades his
heretical discovery that "our constitution has perpetrated
the most damable [*sic*] political theory ever conceived—

namely that men are created equal"; he struts his contempt for "our great Boob Public," a crawling mass of Presbyterians, Rotarians, Boosters, Realtors, etc.; he is proud that usually he can "simply ignore" the "hundred million" around him, "unless they begin to blow their bad breath and their superstitions in my face"; and when he becomes magnanimous he may express a very literary pity, calling upon his mother to admire his "compassion for all the poor blind fumbling Creatures that inhabit this earth." [5] Similarly the first stirrings of social criticism in *Of Time and the River* are personal and youthful. Wolfe's discovery of something jaded, sterile and unwholesome in the world of wealth and fashion reveals as much about him as about

[5] These letters are sometimes rather painful. In his early twenties Wolfe was naturally given to posing for posterity, with a special fondness for set melancholy attitudes: "Proud fool! I have eaten of the Lotus and dreamed too deeply; the world is at me with its long fingers, and must have its payment." But when past twenty-five he may still write as if he were a thousand years old: "I can no longer grow excited over any of the things that ever seemed to me excellent and pleasant and wise." The young Hamlet is no more appealing when he flexes his genius. "I shall be great," runs this refrain, and by God "I shall yet force the inescapable fact down the throats of the rats and vermin who await the proof," and —"if I do not die too soon"—you will be known as my mother. Then the young genius is apt to ask her for money again; he was as untidy in his financial affairs as in his art. All this naïveté is the more prominent because his letters grow shorter and fewer as he grows older.

Nevertheless these letters reveal not only his passion for greatness but the underlying integrity, sensitiveness, humility, and deep feeling for humanity that were the means of experiencing greatness. They bear out his main reason for believing that he was an artist: "The things that really mattered have sunk in and left their mark."

American civilization: the young writer is not only disenchanted but resentful because he is poor and un-
appreciated.

Toward the end of the novel, however, a deeper note is
struck. As Wolfe grows aware that he must seek his image
"in ways stranger, darker, and more painful" than he had
ever dreamed, he begins to look more closely and imper-
sonally at the contradictions in American life. They are
not causeless or caused simply by "human nature." Americans seem lost and they hunger for a better life, as men
naturally do; but they seem unnaturally haunted and hurt
because they feel that they have lost their proper inheritance as Americans, a rich inheritance of exultancy, abundance, and splendor. They have lost it because of "some
foul, corrosive poison in our lives—bitter enigma that it is!"
The depression, however, gave Wolfe some idea of the
nature of this poison. It made the enigma more terrible
but less of an enigma, and therefore not simply bitter. This
idea will become clearer and more explicit in his later
novels. But meanwhile his account of his three years in
Brooklyn gives more weight to the "supreme ecstasy" in
the closing pages of *Of Time and the River*. What might
otherwise appear to be only another chant, or a prelude
to the entrance of the fair Esther—to borrow Fielding's
introduction of Sophia Western, "A short hint of what we
can do in the sublime"—may now be taken as a valid expression of the American dream. It is a happy ending
wrung from the painful experience of all that threatens
the realization of the dream.

Accordingly Wolfe's story of his novel includes a pro-
spectus of the novels to follow. He sees that his "book"

describes two complete cycles: one "the period of wandering and hunger in a man's youth," the other "the period of greater certitude . . . dominated by the unity of a single passion." He has not yet completed the chronicle of the first cycle, but he has himself entered well into the second. In fact, he has already written, though not published, some of the second chronicle. (The manuscript from which *Of Time and the River* was fashioned was entitled *The October Fair* when first delivered to his editor, and was twice as long as *War and Peace*—in other words, about twelve times the length of the average novel.) The "single passion" that is to unify his work is suggested in the admirable statement of his problem as an American artist which concludes *The Story of a Novel*, and which I quoted at the outset (p. 9). As always with Wolfe, we must add qualifications. The statement is very broad; it leaves open the problems of specific content and method, the technical problems that he never mastered; it leaves out the problem (especially for the poet) of finding an audience as well as a tongue. Altogether, Wolfe still has a long way to go, his work is cut out for him. But he now has a clearer vision of the road ahead, and his work is indeed cut out in something like a recognizable artistic shape.

4. TRANSITION

WITH *THE WEB AND THE ROCK*, WOLFE BEGAN ALL OVER again on a new novel, with new characters, under a new editor (Edward C. Aswell). Despite his insistence that all great fiction is deeply autobiographical, he had brooded over the repeated charge that he could write only autobiography, and only with the help of his editor. (Bernard DeVoto in particular had got under his skin.) Now he signaled a kind of declaration of artistic independence by changing his publishers, dropping Eugene Gant, and starting out on the life story of one George "Monk" Webber. "Through free creation," he announces in the Author's Note to the novel, he has sought a release of his "inventive power"; this is the "most objective novel" he has written, and marks a "turning away" from his previous work, "a genuine spiritual and artistic change."

At first glance, this is a ludicrously naïve pretense, the more pathetic because as usual Wolfe was quite sincere, and had high hopes of his new enterprise.[1] He is still writing his autobiography. He has not turned away from his early work but has done it over again, gone back over the same ground. Much of the artistic change is strictly nominal, a matter of names: Eugene Gant becomes George Webber but remains Thomas Wolfe, Altamont becomes Libya Hill but remains Asheville, Eliza's clan of Pentlands become Joyners but remain the clan of Wolfe's maternal ancestors, etc. Some of the conspicuous changes still amount to disguises. Old Gant, for example, is replaced by the much less striking figure of John Webber (and it must have cost Wolfe considerable pain to give him up); but like Gant, Webber comes from Pennsylvania, he scandalizes the neighbors because he drinks and has been divorced, he is somewhat grotesque in appearance— he is in a soberer way the same forlorn stranger in a Southern town. Even Wolfe's new material is essentially familiar. One reason for this enterprise, according to Edward Aswell, is that he recalled important things about his childhood that he had "forgotten" to say in *Look Homeward, Angel*; other things, such as a chapter called "The Butcher," he salvaged from the original manuscript of his first novel. In general, Wolfe had to alter his story considerably, if only because he reduced the substance of *Look Homeward, Angel* and *Of Time and the River* to a few hundred pages; but he suggests an old lady who is

[1] The day before he delivered his manuscript to his publisher, he wrote to me (a virtual stranger) that although "a tremendous labor of writing and revision" still lay before him, he felt "a tremendous amount of comfort and satisfaction as the thing begins to shape up. . . . I have at least articulated a tremendous structure."

95

forced to give up her ancestral home and move into a single room: picking over her trunks of keepsakes, discarding many with a pang, yet hugging as many more to her bosom, unable to give them up.

Likewise Wolfe's "free creations" reveal more about his early life than his new purposes. The first notable character he invented is Nebraska Crane, a sturdy, fearless, imperturbable Cherokee lad who is George Webber's boyhood friend and who grows up to be a big league baseball player. He is a successful creation, as alive as most of the characters Wolfe drew from life. But the artistic reason for this invention is not very clear: Nebraska has no particular influence on George's life, no vital relation to the main theme. The actual reason is suggested by Edward Aswell: he is "the kind of friend the youthful Tom Wolfe always wanted and never had." In other words, he represents a wish-fulfillment. He is comparable to the many women in Wolfe who are described as lovely, tender, sensual, ripe, lavish, "undulant with all the voluptuous maturity of womanhood." [2]

The most genuine artistic change in *The Web and the Rock* itself gives away Wolfe's "new" enterprise. It is a change not in his materials but in his attitude toward them; he relates the early history of George Webber far more coolly and objectively than he had the history of Eugene

[2] This kind of wishfulness receives its most naïve expression in *The Web and the Rock,* in an erotic daydream George is allowed to indulge in about an imaginary affair with a silken lady of wealth. It is given some fifteen pages of voluptuous detail, starting from the moment George is admitted to his lady's mansion by her maid, "a well-made girl of twenty-one or two, who obviously bathed frequently, and who wore expensive black silk stockings—which her mistress gave her—on her heavy but shapely legs."

Gant. Midway in the novel, however, there is an abrupt break. George has seemed like an ordinary young man, enjoying himself in college and in New York; then, suddenly, he boils over with hunger and fury, turns into Eugene Gant. The last half of the novel is centered on his love affair with Mrs. Esther Jack, an affair which is again drawn directly from Wolfe's own life. Wolfe had not only introduced Esther at the end of *Of Time and the River* but had completed the story of their love in his old vein, for his original purposes, before conceiving his new project. From here on he is simply continuing the legend outlined in *The Story of a Novel*. Because he felt spiritually changed, he decided to make a fresh start; but because his central theme was the same, and much of the later chronicle already written, his new introduction could not be substantially new. George Webber would have to be like Eugene Gant because he had to become Eugene Gant. His early life could differ only superficially because it had to lead to the same maturity, or immaturity. In short, the first half of *The Web and the Rock* was merely grafted on to Wolfe's original legend; and the grafting is a rather crude job. The result is the least impressive of his novels.

Yet the result might have been quite different had Wolfe not died. When *The Web and the Rock* appeared, it was advertised as the first of two novels that he had completed before his untimely death; so it was the more disappointing to readers who had been excited by the promise of *The Story of a Novel*. Actually, Wolfe had not completed these novels. As usual, he had delivered to his publishers a huge pile of manuscript, as a preliminary to the "tremendous labor of writing and revision" that was part of his routine.

97

From this manuscript his editor fashioned two novels as best he could, supplying brief continuity to fill some gaps. Had Wolfe lived, he would almost certainly have made considerable changes as well as additions. It was not his habit to tinker, or merely revise passages that did not satisfy him; he would rewrite entire. In particular, he would have reworked the love story, with which he was not at all satisfied. He told Aswell that he wanted another year to rewrite it.

As the novels stand, the sequel, *You Can't Go Home Again,* is by far the better. It is more nearly finished, and almost all of it is in Wolfe's mature manner. *The Web and the Rock* is a transitional work, uncertain in intention and uneven in accomplishment. Not only does it break into two different parts, but the last half in turn is an incomplete fusion of two versions of the love affair. The original version was a complete defense of Eugene Gant; Wolfe altered portions of it, to expose George Webber in a much less agreeable light, but did not revise it thoroughly. Nevertheless he was in fact undergoing a spiritual change and attempting an artistic change, striving earnestly for impersonality and restraint. His efforts were not wholly successful, nor wholly unsuccessful; they entailed both gains and losses. As a transitional work, *The Web and the Rock* makes an interesting text for the study of Wolfe's growth.

2

Since the last half of the novel is largely in Wolfe's early manner, it is convenient to ignore the pretended continuity and begin in the middle with Book IV, "The Magic

Year"; for here we pick up the hero where *Of Time and the River* left him. George Webber, né Eugene Gant, is on a great liner in the month of August, 1925, shortly before his twenty-fifth birthday. He is returning to his position as English instructor at New York University, now called the School for Utility Cultures, Inc. (In the Author's Note, Wolfe announces that his novel "has in it, from first to last, a strong element of satiric exaggeration.") When he lands in New York, the "supreme ecstasy" of the homecoming is quickly succeeded by his old feeling of homelessness. The immortal city is the "most homeless home" on earth, the "gigantic tenement of Here Comes Everybody" (or Howth Castle and Environs, Haveth Childers Everywhere, Humphrey Chimpden Earwicker—the H.C.E. of *Finnegans Wake*). Nevertheless this is to be a magic year, which will afford him supreme ecstasies of another kind. On the boat he meets Mrs. Esther Jack, a middle-aged woman with a fresh, rosy, jolly little face, a fine, warm talent as a stage-designer, and as natural a talent for the art of living in joy, beauty and love. After they fall in love, George continues to teach and to write, in Eugene's habitual anguish of spirit; but the rest of the novel is devoted chiefly to his relations with Esther over the next three years.

It is a strange love affair, clouded almost from the beginning by George's ugly suspicions, and soon becoming a violent alternation of rapture and resentment. It is not one of the great love stories in fiction. Wolfe records all too faithfully the natural extravagances of rapture, which are apt to sound silly to the unenraptured observer ("I like her face, and I like her pace, and I like her grace!"), and which are the less luminous because they are usually touched off by the cry of "Food! Food! Food!"—the steak, salad, or onion soup that Esther is preparing for George. The stormy scenes, on the other hand, make painful reading; George's treatment of Esther is often so vile, obscene, that one writhes. The whole story belongs to the first cycle of Wolfe's legend, "the period of wandering and hunger in a man's youth." He tells it with his usual honesty but without complete understanding, much less delicacy or subtlety. Again he exposes a great deal, explains somewhat less. The episode is more interesting for its autobiographical revelations than for its artistic meanings, and these revelations are to a considerable extent unconscious.

Wolfe does relate this affair to the main theme of his pilgrimage. Esther is not merely a lovely woman with whom George conceivably might find happiness; she is in a deeper sense the woman of his dreams—the dreams of the lost country boy, the stranger from the lonely hills, the writer who is seeking a tongue, a door, a home. "In some curious way," he realized, "the woman had come to represent 'the city' to him." She was the "city's daughter," who completely "belonged"; she was wealthy and secure, moved freely among the fashionable and the famous, knew intimately all the enchantments of the "magic island." Through her, George came really to know the city he had longed to enter. But he did not belong. He found this world idle, sterile, cynical, depraved—profoundly hostile to the arts it patronized or exploited. And Esther, the symbol of the fabulous rock of Manhattan, was also a symbol of this infamous web of corruption. Despite her freshness, warmth, health and high integrity, her allegiances were mixed; she was loyal to this worldly society as well as to the world of creative work. "She was a part of this thing, too—of this Midas world of night, of this reptilian wink, its criminal corruption and inhuman privilege, the impregnable arrogance of its living sneer." Esther provides the text for an explicit sermon on Wolfe's new theme of social injustice:

> It was a world that seemed to have gone insane with its own excess, a world of criminal privilege that flouted itself with an inhuman arrogance in the very face of a great city where half the population lived in filth and squalor, and where two-thirds were still so bitterly uncertain of their daily living that they had to thrust, to snarl, to curse, to cheat, contrive, and get the better of their fellows like a race of mongrel dogs. . . . Meanwhile, these blind men lived in filth and went through a daily struggle just to get the barest means of life, and they swallowed down obediently all the vicious nonsense that any politician told them about the 'high standard' of their living which, these wretches were solemnly assured, made them 'the envy of the world.'

Hence George's ultimate break with Esther represents Wolfe's break with this world of his youthful dreams.

All this is very pertinent to Wolfe's myth, if unfair to Esther. Yet these symbolical meanings hardly justify his extended treatment of the love affair. They were plain enough before the affair began; in *Of Time and the River* he had already treated fully his disillusionment with the world of wealth and fashion. Moreover, he often forgets these meanings, dwelling on personal detail for its own sake, and then seems to drag them in as rationalizations. They do not constitute the whole meaning, or even the primary meaning, of the affair as it is actually dramatized by Wolfe. A more apparent reason for George's break with

Esther is simply that she was almost twice his age—a reason easy to understand, but not easy to make symbolically significant. Another is his resentment of his dependence upon her, which was heightened by envy of her sure talent. (Wolfe had a similar feeling towards his mother, upon whose care he had also depended.) Still other reasons, however, are not so apparent. Wolfe himself stresses the irrationality and perversity of George's behavior. George is tortured by the conviction that he is throwing away the finest thing that he ever had or can ever hope to have. He had searched "the faces of a million people to see if there was one who was as jolly, fresh, and fair as she, to see if there was one who had an atom of her loveliness, a glimmer of the glorious richness, joy, and noble beauty that showed in every act and visage of her life, and there was no one he had ever seen who could compare with her." Why, he asks himself, has he shamefully betrayed not only Esther but himself, foully dishonored not only love but life itself? What enemy had worked this evil? And Wolfe goes to medieval mythology to suggest an answer:

> He could not find a tongue for his bewilderment, but he now felt with unutterable certitude the presence of a demon of perverse denial which was, and was everywhere, abroad throughout the universe, and at work forever in the hearts of men. It was the cunning, subtle cheat, the mocker of life, the scourger of time; and man, with the full glory and the tragic briefness of his days before him in his sight, bowed like a dull slave before the thief that looted him of all his joy, and held him sullen but submissive to its evil wizardry.

This "demon" is not sheer nonsense. It may be regarded as a symbol of the tragic contradictions within man which indeed poison his happiness, or cause him to destroy his loves; in Wolfe it is another name for his insatiable, all-consuming hunger. But this symbol is hardly consistent with Wolfe's other symbolism, which would make his final rejection of Esther a triumph over the insidious corruption of the city—in effect, a kind of happy ending.[3] Hence the love story points finally to the contradictions in Wolfe himself. It is not a representative "American" love story; an artist consciously designing an American legend or myth would invent a quite different story. Rather, it illustrates all the callow, perverse, morbid attitudes that Wolfe had to outgrow before he could write his American legend.

These attitudes were strictly morbid—Wolfe did not fully realize how dangerous an enemy his demon was. At this stage the frustration of the struggling young writer in the city had developed into a feeling of persecution that approached downright mania. All around him he saw not merely indifference but hatred, malice, venom—a calculated plot to destroy him. He had to have enemies; nothing else could explain his frustrations. He had made Starwick his "mortal enemy" because Starwick had got the woman he wanted. Now that he himself has won a woman he makes her the enemy. "The enemy had come, but not as he expected him," George thinks in his self-inflicted torment; though he has often been unfaithful to Esther, the groundless suspicion that she may be unfaithful to him convinces him that he has suffered "a defeat, a humiliation, a ruin more horrible and irrevocable" than he had known in his

[3] There is a similar confusion in the symbolism of the "web" in his title. In the last half of the novel it is the web of corruption; in the first half it is the quite different web of George's childhood, comparable to "the web of earth."

103

nightmares. Worse, she has shorn him of his strength, his faith, his energy, his genius—she has "sapped and gutted" him. Simply to stave off for a few years the approach of age and death, she has used up his glorious youth, and joined the fiendish conspiracy of all her rich, impotent, cynical, corrupt friends who lie awake nights plotting in order that "the good man—the real artist—the true poet— should be done to death."

In this mania, all the vulgar prejudices of the provincial are luridly exposed. George begins to feel a "bitter mistrust" when a somber, brooding look occasionally transforms Esther's jolly face. He cannot understand the secret of this look: "He felt tricked and cheated and baffled by a cleverness and subtlety of living that was too old, too wise and crafty, for him to fathom or contend with." Presently he wants to cry out furiously, "What is the meaning of this tragic and mysterious air? Do you think you are so subtle I cannot understand you? You're not so wonderful as all that! I have thoughts and feelings just as deep as yours!" So, too, with all her sophisticated, fine-feathered friends: they're not so deep and fine as he is, even if he is poor and unknown. So, in particular, with all her Jewish relatives and friends. George is fascinated by their opulence and sensuality, their dark pride and patience, their ancient subtlety and wisdom, and especially their lavish women and their rich food—Esther's surest method of appeasement is to serve him some Jewish food, reminding him of the tasteless Christian cookery. But he also resents their opulence, fears their cunning, hates their assurance and knowingness. Wolfe's callow prejudice flares up in some of his ugliest passages as George reviles the "proud and potent beak-nosed Jews," the "rich Park Avenue Jews," the sly, crafty Jews who "had used Esther as a bait to snare the yokel"—as their ancestors had used Queen Esther.

All this fester is brought to a head by the completion of George Webber's first novel (in other words, of *Look Homeward, Angel*). The first publishers to whom he submits the manuscript, at Esther's suggestion, are not impressed by its power—they are merely appalled by its bulk. They did not even read it, Wolfe says; and there is an evident bitterness in his caricature of these publishers, the firm of "Rawng and Wright." As might be expected, at any rate, his hero experiences the natural emotions with preternatural intensity. He takes them all out on Esther. She is a Jewish harpy who feeds on young men; she is a rotten Park Avenue bitch, worse than a gutter whore. Nor is she any happier for George's remorse. "He who repents," Spinoza said, "is twice unhappy and doubly weak." As George repents, he turns all his violence upon himself; and hating himself more, he then hates her more.

Love is not enough, George concludes. This kind of love is too much, one might add. But even after discounting possible exaggeration, and the fever of this crisis in his career, one may point to a personal limitation in the young Wolfe that is reflected in his early novels. He was incapable of a steady love, unequal to the responsibilities of any close bond. "For Eugene Gant," John Peale Bishop remarked discerningly, "the only satisfactory relationship with another human creature is one which can have no continuity." Eugene is often filled with compassionate understanding when he views people from a distance (especially from the window of a train); then he can love and

105

pity Man. But when he comes close enough to overhear these same people, when he is forced to jostle elbows with men, he is apt to feel only bitterness, hatred, or disgust. Likewise he breaks off his closest relationships, with Starwick as with Esther, because he is unequal to a continuous claim on his sentiment, resentful of his feeling of dependence—and also, perhaps, because in the homosexual and the aging woman, alike loving and lovable but now frustrate, he unconsciously sees his own frustration. The one bond he cannot escape is that with his family, but neither can he live with them; his love for them is not a steady warmth but an intermittent blaze, alternating with as blazing a resentment; he treats them most sympathetically when he is away from them; and the one he loves best is the lonely, loveless Ben—in whose death, Bishop suggests, he sees his own fate. Eugene's inability to maintain a deeply satisfying relation with any one person helps to explain his passion to know a million people. Because he could not completely or consistently experience the Biblical wisdom that "two are better than one," he had to believe that a million were better than two.

Altogether, Esther gives an apt account of the mind of her lover:

"Now," she thought, "I know exactly what he's thinking. There are still a few things in the universe which have not been arranged to suit his pleasure, so he wants to see them changed. And his desires are modest, aren't they? . . . All he wants is to eat his cake and keep on having it forever. He's tired of me and he wishes I would go away and leave him here alone to contemplate his navel. He also wishes I would stay here with him. I am the one he loves, his jolly little Jew that he adores and could devour, and I am also the evil wench who lies in wait for unsuspecting country boys. I am the joy and glory of his life, and I am also the sinister and corrupt harpy who has been employed by the forces of darkness to kill and destroy his life. And why? Why, because he is so innocent and pure . . . and all the rotten people who hate life are staying up at night plotting how to wreck and ruin him. The Jews hate the Christians, and they also love them. The Jewish women seduce the pure young Christian boys because they love them and want to destroy them, and the Jewish men, cynical and resigned, look on and rub their hands in glee because they hate the Christians and also love them, too, and want to destroy them because they love to see them suffer, but really adore them because they feel such sympathy and pity for them, and yet say nothing because they get an obscene sexual satisfaction from the spectacle, and because their souls are old and patient, and they have known that their women were unfaithful for seven thousand years, and they must suffer and endure it. Weave! Weave! Weave! He weaves it day and night out of his crazy and tormented brain until not even Einstein could make head or tail of it—and yet he thinks it all as plain and clear as day!

Here, however, we come to an important distinction. It is Wolfe who writes this devastating account of George Webber; so he is not to be identified with George. Throughout the affair he allows Esther to be eloquent in her own defense. Although he also allows George to rehearse his charges against her with more passion and eloquence than are called for, and perhaps sympathizes too much with George's jealousy of her mixed allegiances, we must remember that he rewrote only parts of the love story and wanted to rewrite the rest. But even as it stands he treats George more harshly (at least in the opinion of masculine critics) than does Aline Bernstein, who tells the same unhappy story from Esther's point of view in *The Journey Down*. She is less insistent upon the savagery of her nameless hero, and she attributes to him not only a

107

"mighty nature" but a "beauty and sweetness" that one seldom feels in George.[4] If anything, Wolfe is too pitiless in his exposure of George. He is writing with the terrible truthfulness that makes it impossible to tell the exact or the whole truth, for which pity or love might also be needed.

In general, this affair is comparable to the different but

[4] One incidental discrepancy in the two versions is of interest to the amateur psychologist. Both report that the first date of the lovers, a celebration of the hero's twenty-fifth birthday, gets off to a bad start because one is an hour late for the appointment; both have him greeting her with the remark that she looks swell in brown. But Wolfe has Esther arriving late, Mrs. Bernstein makes the hero the tardy one. Other differences are chiefly in emphasis. Mrs. Bernstein writes in something like the manner of Virginia Woolf, confining herself to the consciousness of her heroine; she succeeds in conveying vivid impressions of the hero, but not in creating a full-bodied character. Perhaps most vivid are somewhat amusing aspects of his intensity that Wolfe himself was too intense to do justice to. This is how he began to make love when they first met on the boat:

"He talked, he asked her about herself, what she had been do-ing all these years, what her life was like, what she wore, how many pairs of shoes she had, how many nightgowns and dresses and wrappers, what her clothing cost a year, what her room was like, what her house was like, what books she read, what poetry she loved, all the time bruising her with his thoughtless strength, his excitement and passion rising with the drinks of heady brandy. He asked her if she could cook, if she would cook for him, if she was a low immoral woman, he asked her if she was good, he told her she could not be good, she must be vile if she spent her life in the theatre, he told her he was running away, that he had run away all over France to forget a girl he loved who had treated him badly, to forget a false friend, he was running away from the knife-thrusts of those he had trusted, from friends who had tricked him and laughed behind his back."

Mrs. Bernstein has said that Wolfe expressed a high opinion of her novel.

no less excruciating love affair in Somerset Maugham's *Of Human Bondage*. Like Maugham, Wolfe told this story in order to rid himself of a humiliating memory. Both the man of the world and the small-town American used their readers for the very simple human purpose of getting something off their chests; and their readers may feel a little uncomfortable, as one is apt to when listening to confessions. Neither spared himself.

By this comparison Wolfe again appears artless and extravagant. He is closer to his affair, recollecting in less tranquillity; he remembers more vividly but comprehends less clearly; he is remorselessly intense where Maugham is remorselessly analytical. In particular, he lacks a clear artistic design. Maugham's painful love story is the climactic illustration of the main theme of his novel, "of human bondage" to passions; it is a definite turning point in his hero's career, a logical, dramatic means to his ultimate freedom. Wolfe's love story, once more, seems like an incidental episode, a natural but not artistically necessary part of the hero's experience. At the end, his hero as naturally recovers from his mad passion; he flees to Europe, wanders restlessly and finally, after a drunken brawl that lands him in the hospital, looks "calmly and sanely forth upon the earth for the first time in ten years." His recovery, however, also seems more like an epilogue than a dramatic resolution; the sketchy travelogue that concludes the novel is a kind of perfunctory musical accompaniment to a drama whose issue is stated but not rendered.

Yet the recovery was real. Wolfe had largely solved his emotional or spiritual problems, if not his technical ones; and the last word should be given to the marked change in his attitude toward his hero. It was "vitally important to the success of this book," he wrote Aswell, "that there be no trace of Eugene Gant-iness in the character of the protagonist," no "romantic self-justification." He was not, then, wholly successful in the book as he left it. George Webber still has Eugene's voice, his hunger, his fury and some of his habits, such as his bloody knuckle smashing; and at times his author still sympathizes with such behavior.[5] Nevertheless these traces of romantic self-justification are not so much a lingering hangover in Wolfe himself as relics of the original Gant story. Even though a Eugene Gant dies pretty hard, we may fairly assume that had Wolfe lived to rewrite the story thoroughly, Eugene would have been killed for good. For he rewrote enough to make plain that, like Maugham, he was no longer in bondage to his youthful passions. Hence he is able to do full justice to Esther, in truth and in pity. He not only pays tribute to her radiant beauty and goodness but pays her the highest compliment of making her radiantly alive and thoroughly convincing. Esther is among Wolfe's most memorable creations. As she fights wildly, uselessly against the passing of youth and love, waging ugly war with George, she is not only pitiable but tragic. Even George sees dignity in her refusal to resign herself to the inevitable:

He knew that she was right, and would be right if she went to her grave with a curse of wild denial on her lips, because such

[5] Wolfe also preserves his physical abnormality. Where Eugene had been huge, George is given extremely long arms, a torso too large and heavy for his short legs and other simian features that earn him the nickname of "Monk." He is "not really grotesque," Wolfe adds; but he is abnormal enough to stand out in a crowd—and like Eugene to resent the laughter and surprise he occasions.

beauty, courage, love, and youth, and strength as she had known should not grow old, and should never die, and that truth was with her, no matter how inevitable the triumph of this all-devouring, all-victorious enemy.

This note Wolfe now strikes repeatedly. In sadness, in ecstasy and in awe he celebrates the "unshaken and magnificent resolution of little man," who is more than man and less than spirit; who is strong, great and brave because he is so weak, small and full of fear; who gazes, desolate, into the illimitable and everlasting darkness and finds no answer, knows that there is no answer, but gives his own defiant answer. Wolfe has transcended his familiar anguish over "the bitter briefness of our days" and now feels at once the glory and the pathos of mortality. When his senses take him out of himself, out of the present, he is carried beyond the lost America of his youth to a vision of all human destiny, the everlasting life-in-death, with its fabric of youth, love and beauty that can never die, and that are dying with every breath we draw. He embraces "the whole passionate enigma of life, the living contradiction, the undemonstrable but overwhelming unity which comprises every antithesis by which men live and die"; and then he utters "the goat-cry of exultant joy and ecstasy torn from the heart of ageless grief and tragic destiny."

This theme is as old as the hills. Wolfe's language is also full of echoes of the tragic poets, from Sophocles and Ecclesiastes to Shakespeare and Melville. Nevertheless it does not seem like borrowed finery or straining for profundity. The consistent stress on good-in-evil, in a relatively sober tone, implies that Wolfe has come to accept the universe. He has achieved the reconciliation of oppo-sites which Coleridge believed was essential to great art.

3

At the end of *The Web and the Rock* George Webber-Wolfe has learned, through sweat and blood, what simple men know from the outset: that he loved life and his fellowmen, and that it was better to live than to die. He has learned "that a spirit which thinks itself too fine for the rough uses of the world is too young and callow, or else too centered on itself, too inward-turning, too en-amored of the beauties of its own artistic soul and worth to find itself by losing self in something larger than itself, and thus to find its place and do a man's work in the world —too fine for all of this, and hence defeated, precious, fit for nothing." It is this new Wolfe who wrote the first half of *The Web and the Rock*.

He is unquestionably much calmer and saner. Although he may still grow iambic, he no longer writes hymns to fury. His hero is not given to seething; his emotions are generally utterable, tolerable, exorable. George Webber is a more or less normal youngster who broods but who also enjoys circuses, plays baseball, climbs trees and exer-cises his muscles as well as his nerves.[6] His experience in college is typical of Wolfe's metamorphosis. Eugene Gant won prizes and honors, but we see him chiefly as a tense, lonely, scornful student—rather unlike Wolfe himself, who

[6] Edward Aswell states that for a while Wolfe called his hero Joe Doaks—in an excess of humility, I assume. We may be great-ful that he finally decided upon the name of Webber when he began toying with the symbolism of "The Web and the Rock."

from all accounts was busy, popular and happy in fraternity life and the various extra-curricular activities by which college men mold their characters and get well-rounded. George Webber is a serious student, deeply interested in literature, but otherwise he seems typical enough. We follow him to Richmond for the big football game of the season, when "Pine Rock" beats "Monroe and Madison" for the first time in nine years. "How to tell the wonder and glory of that trip?" Wolfe writes.

In fact, however, he does not succeed in telling it very well; the trip is far more thrilling for George than for the reader; and the unfortunate truth is that Wolfe's sanity does not always become him or make him a better writer. At times he is calm to the point of banality. Of Old Catawba he writes, "But really when you know the place and think about it more and more its name is wonderful." Or his efforts at restraint may betray him into a schoolmarm style. To be "dressed up," he states, is a healthy and invigorating experience; then he immediately repeats, "To be formally attired for the first time in the conventional appointments of society is one of the memorable experiences in a man's life." And these occasional lapses reveal more than uneasiness in an unaccustomed manner. Wolfe's second account of his youth is relatively dispirited. He was exuberant about the idea of his new enterprise, the idea of being free, but he was not so happy in its execution, or really free.

Thus, when he condenses into a couple of hundred pages what had first taken almost a thousand, we cannot simply praise him for a first brave effort at economy. The truth is that even his memory was not inexhaustible; he had used up most of his best material, and was unable to invent anything as good. Accordingly the effect of his condensation is not density but sketchiness and scrappiness. The first hundred pages of *The Web and the Rock* are chiefly generalized narrative, a kind of autobiographical essay, in which he seldom dramatizes a scene. "The bare anatomy of the story runs as follows," Wolfe says in introducing the history of John Webber; and too often he runs on without bothering to flesh out the bare anatomy of his narrative. From time to time he generalizes even his sensory memories, presenting a mere inventory of smells, sounds, sights, feels—a prosaic summary rather than a poetic condensation, and so a duller kind of excess. In general, one often misses Wolfe's characteristic rich flavor in this warmed-over history.

In particular, one misses the Gant family. Because John Webber deserted his wife, who presently died, to live with another woman, young George lives with his Aunt Maw Joyner; and there is no replacement for the family group that provided the magnificent scenes of *Look Homeward, Angel*. To Aunt Maw, Wolfe gives the voice of Eliza, so that she may continue to weave the history of the Joyner clan in rich monologues; but except for the voice she is a pale, shadowy version of Eliza. John Webber is vivid enough but still an inferior substitute for Will Gant, and he is not given a fair chance anyway; he appears in no dramatic scenes. There are no brothers or sisters to take the place of Ben, Helen and Luke. Nor was Wolfe seeking here to improve upon his original artistic design; he eliminated the Gants primarily to save his own family further

114

embarrassment. Hence one is startled when George's shadowy Uncle Mark Joyner suddenly turns into something like Eugene's Uncle Bascom, in a scene orchestrated in Wolfe's old manner. To the "demented howling" of "maniacal winds" under a "savage sky"—amid a hail of tympanic adjectives, which stir up a "wild, wordless, and unutterable" state in George—Mark sneers, snarls and howls a curse upon the memory of his father. It goes on for ten pages and is quite extravagant; but most readers will be grateful for it.

Altogether, Wolfe's new introduction to his legend is scarcely an improvement on *Look Homeward, Angel.* Yet it is not simply regrettable. It contains a number of notable characters and scenes, including a few that are notably good in a new manner. "The Child by Tiger," for example —a chapter on a religious negro who suddenly goes berserk and is tracked down after a wild shooting spree—is excellent narrative in a sharply objective style; Wolfe allows the story to make its own point. And other alterations and innovations, though revealing no remarkable artistry, indicate that he now has a clearer artistic design.

One change is a different attitude toward his father. The childhood of Eugene Gant was a confused battleground of fierce, ambiguous loyalties and rebellions; he was deeply attached to both his father and his mother, and deeply resented both. The childhood of George Webber is savagely divided but clearly divided; he consciously identifies himself with his father from whom he is separated. The dark, fatal world of his mother's clan—the "ever-perfect, doom-prophetic, horror-hungry, time-devouring Joyners"—is also in his blood and bone, but this is the enemy, the "bad" world.[7] The "good" world is the world of his father, with its "sinful warmth and radiance." His father is godless and immoral, but he knows happiness and he is strong and solid—a builder whose life-long motto is that the only way to build is with brick and stone, as men do in his native Pennsylvania. And so George's spirit "flamed beyond the hills, beyond lost time and sorrow, to his father and his father's earth," and to the shining city of the North.

This shift may be regarded as Wolfe's belated recognition of his deepest allegiance, and a belated penitential offering. As a son he was closer to his mother, but as an artist he was closer to his father, the source of his hunger, his passion and his eloquence. "There has never been anybody like Papa," he wrote home after his father's death. Yet Wolfe had left home for Boston knowing that his father was dying. "I foresee these consequences," he wrote his mother at the time. "Do you think they have not been gouged in my very soul?" Now, at last, he makes amends for his desertion. Occasionally he even has George Webber talk like old Gant ("Jesus God! That it should come to this!"); and one of the most violent scenes with Esther follows when, in defending her people, she jeers at George's father—though the father she pictures is more like Gant than John Webber. To complete his variant of the Oedipus myth, Wolfe symbolically kills Eliza by having Aunt Maw die. He had long been dependent on his

[7] The ethos of the Pentland-Joyners is neatly summarized by Eliza's comment, in "The Web of Earth," on a mountaineer who was a notorious killer but never ran around after women: "They had to give the devil his due—his morals were pure."

TRANSITION

mother, and haunted by the knowledge that she did not really approve of his way of life or understand his work; in helping him financially she was being indulgent to her youngest child, who had been a "very beautiful baby," who as a boy had had "beautiful curls" that she curled every day, and who had slept with her until he was a "great big boy." [8] For all her vitality and her indomitable spirit, she represented the provincial attitudes that he found intolerable.

Artistically, at any rate, Wolfe's new conception brings into sharper focus his father-symbol. In the early novels his symbolism is cloudy; he does not come to grips with the relationship of the father and the son. Eugene's blind hunger for a nameless happiness, which he called the quest of a father, an image of strength and wisdom, might also have been called the quest of a mother, an image of warmth and love. But now the father represents all that the hero has been deprived of and yearns for. The conflict is more sharply defined, the issue brought to a head.

Accordingly the related themes of the hero's pilgrimage are also stated and developed more consciously. From the outset of *The Web and the Rock*, Wolfe dwells on the theme of the South: the "world-lost and hill-haunted sorrow" of the Joyners; the "heart of darkness" out of which come the negro who goes berserk, and the white men who lynch negroes; the suspicion, hatred, cruelty and lust that are rooted in fear, the "tortured and envenomed terror"

[8] I quote from Mrs. Wolfe's account of his childhood, in John Terry's introduction to *Thomas Wolfe's Letters to His Mother*. Wolfe himself often quoted her remark when he told her that he had sold a story for $1500: "Boy, you're the only one in the family who can make that much money without working."

of the old, stricken South. He continues to satirize the decadent aristocracy, with its provinciality, its cherished illusion of what it used to be, its chivalry that is so lofty because it is so often groundless or merely verbal. In his new social consciousness, he explicitly contrasts all this romantic mythology with the squalid realities of the bondage of negroes, of tenant farmers, of the children working fourteen hours a day in cotton mills. He also turns his attack on the Southern intellectuals and esthetes, the "lily-handed" cultists who, in academic security, were celebrating "the agrarian way of life" in a language that few actual agrarians could understand. He sums up the whole traditional code as a "rationalizing self-defense of Southern fear and Southern failure: its fear of conflict and of competition in the greater world; its inability to meet or to adjust itself to the conditions, strifes and ardors of a modern life; its old, sick, Appomattoxlike retreat into the shades of folly and delusion, of prejudice and bigotry, of florid legend and defensive casuistry, of haughty and ironic detachment from a life with which it was too obviously concerned, to which it wished too obviously to belong."

Wolfe's attitude toward the South is still ambivalent, however, or even slightly ambiguous. To Old Catawba he remains loyal; its people are "just common, plain, and homely—but almost everything of America is in them." The Joyners, apparently, are not really representative. He also finds warmth, depth and richness in the dark heart of the South; its romantic legend is not, after all, simply a hollow pretense. He ridicules all the Southerners in the North who proclaim passionately the superiority of Southern culture and seem eager to bleed and die in its name—"to do

almost everything, in fact, for dear old Dixie except to return permanently to her to live"; yet he adds that the
North should be grateful for the warmth, the passion, the
energy, the high aspiration and honorable pride they
brought with them. Wolfe's criticism is also somewhat subtler. In admiring the real gallantry of the spirited, imaginative Southerners, he notes: "It is admirable to win against
terrific odds, but it is not admirable, not well for the health
and endurance of the spirit, to be able to win only against
terrific odds." But the upshot of all this is the same. To find
himself, George Webber needs a larger, freer, airier world;
so upon graduating from college, he leaves the South for
good.

Here Wolfe gives more prominence to the theme of the
country boy in the big city. In *Of Time and the River* this
theme is blurred by the Harvard episode; after his exciting
train ride, Eugene Gant associates chiefly with his fellow-
students and his Uncle Bascom, and is concerned only incidentally with the life of Boston. George Webber goes
straight to New York, the shining city of his dreams. As the
train approaches it, he is intoxicated even by the fragrance
of glue factories and by his first glimpse of the heights of
Jersey City, with their garbage dumps. (It may be a little
hard for readers acquainted with Jersey City to thrill to
Wolfe's celebration of these heights, "raised proudly
against the desolation of those lonely marshes as a token of
man's fortitude, a symbol of his power, a sign of his indomitable spirit that flames forever like a great torch in the
wilderness," etc.) Still intoxicated, George sets about
learning the great city and making his way there. Wolfe
amplifies the theme—"one of the most tremendous and vi-

119

tal experiences in the life of a man, and in the life of the nation"—by providing some young Southern friends to share
George's glorious adventure.

In time, naturally, George's ardor cools. He becomes
aware of the impermanence of life on the enfabled rock; he
grows weary of the endless pavements, the incessant
change, the swarming crowds; he is sickened by the gray-
ness, meagerness, sourness of the rock-dwellers. Yet he is
not so violently disillusioned as was Eugene Gant (at least
until he meets Esther and takes over Eugene's role). The
splendor of the city is no illusion. It is a "proud, passionate
Northern place," where everything is vertical, sharp, hard
and bright; it is also magical and mysterious, often overwhelming in its loneliness; and "there is no place like it, no
place with an atom of its glory, pride, and exultancy."
Wolfe is more disposed to accept the incongruities that
link it with the enigma of the savage, tender, meager and
magnificent life of the nation.

Other innovations in this more objective history likewise
sharpen its point. One example is the introduction of
Gerald Alsop, a college friend. Alsop is a fat, genial senti-
mentalist who shares his warm love of literature with
an admiring circle, including George Webber; he loves the
"wholesome and well-rounded view of life" that he finds
especially in Dickens at his shallowest. George is cast out
when he develops an enthusiasm for the "morbid" novels
of Dostoyevsky and the other great Russians. Here Wolfe
dramatizes the literary discoveries and conflicts through
which he formed his own purposes as a writer, and went
his lonely way. Another example is the creation of Jim
Randolph, the leader of George's little group of Southern-

ers in New York. A football hero and a war hero, dashing, generous and vain, Randolph is a shining leader who always has to be a leader, because he can shine only by the adoration of satellites. He grows embittered by the realization that he has become merely a legend, a heroic remnant of an outmoded generation; less than thirty years old, he has lived too long. He accordingly belongs with the many lost souls who bear out Wolfe's central theme of lost America. More specifically, however, he belongs with the "lost generation." He is a product of his times, and points to Wolfe's increasing concern with the specific causes of American lostness.

All these intentions, it must be added, still do not emerge clearly enough from the history of George Webber's early life. The history is too sketchy, episodic, desultory—a miscellany of old memories and new designs; and the form and point are further blurred in the abrupt transformation of George into Eugene Gant in love. By itself, *The Web and the Rock* remains an unsatisfying novel: a whole which is not greater than the sum of its parts, in which the best parts do not gain by their relation to the whole. At best it is still "promising." But it was not designed to stand by itself, at least in its present form. It does gain when placed in a larger whole, Wolfe's entire "book." For in *You Can't Go Home Again* the promise was largely fulfilled.

5. THE END OF THE ROAD

WHEN GEORGE WEBBER RETURNS FROM EUROPE, CURED OF HIS mad passion, he also returns to Esther—the one thing he was sure he would never do. *You Can't Go Home Again* opens with George back in New York, in the spring of 1929, brooding darkly over this inconsistency between his thought and his behavior, seeking comfort in the reflection of a wiser man than he, that "a foolish consistency is the hobgoblin of little minds." Yet he is really cured. He is living his own life in his own apartment, keeping love a thing apart and managing alone his world of writing. He broods quietly, in the awareness that his inconsistencies are natural and typical, not unfathomable or intolerable. He knows and accepts his limitations, having learned at last that he is "the son and brother of all men living," that he cannot devour the earth and have it too, and that the simple word for his wild, wordless torment of the years past was growing pains. He can appreciate that he has learned a good deal even as he wonders why he had not always known something so obvious. And though Eugene Gant had come to have such sober thoughts, with George they have become a settled way of thinking and feeling; his wild moods are now the exception. No longer in bondage to his passions, he is happier than he had ever been.

More important, his creator is now happier in his new enterprise. He had had to go back over old ground, but at this point he is caught up and can at last enter the second cycle of his legend, "the period of greater certitude." Here he can directly portray the spiritual change in himself, prove his new art. To be sure, Wolfe's legend is still personal. The main characters of *You Can't Go Home Again* are drawn from his own experience, and some of the secondary characters are fragments of his early creations. (In Margaret Shepperton, for example, he preserves the physique and affectionate qualities of Helen Gant; in Mrs. Delia Flood he again resurrects Eliza—the voice and manner of the acquisitive Eliza who boasts about her real estate deals.) But Wolfe is no longer a slave to his experience. He is able to make relatively free, impersonal use of these autobiographical materials.

The subdued manner that marks this impersonality is still not a clear gain. There are flat stretches when one feels not so much an effort at restraint as a mechanical, low-powered effortlessness, an unrestrained habit of writing; [1]

[1] Here is a sample: "There is something good in the way people welcome success, or anything—no matter what—that is stamped with the markings of success. It is not an ugly thing, really. People love success because to most of them it means happiness, and, whatever form it takes, it is the image of what they, in their hearts, would like to be. This is more true in America than anywhere else. People put this label on the image of their heart's de-

there is a good deal of respectable, workmanlike prose that lacks the lift and glow as well as the shagginess of his early prose-poetry; in general, there are grounds for preferring the untamed Wolfe, choosing to put up with the bombast and bathos for the sake of the blazing intensity and power. Nevertheless Wolfe has by no means grown afraid to be poetical. There are also many strongly cadenced passages in something like his old vein, generally less impassioned and spontaneous, but generally more varied in their rhythm and imagery, and finer in texture.[2] Had he completed the novel himself, he might have brightened up the prosy stretches.

In technique, however, the gains are clearer. Although hardly a brilliant craftsman, Wolfe is now more flexible and resourceful, able to do more things about a given situation. He naturally continues to present his narrative largely from his hero's point of view, but he keeps a greater distance, he has himself a clear view of George, and he is able to move around freely. Occasionally he gets behind other characters in order to give a different perspective or add another dimension. Chapters on the early morning

sire because they have never had an image of another kind of happiness. So, essentially, this love of success is not a bad thing, but a good thing. It calls forth a general and noble response, even though the response may also be mixed with self-interest. People are happy for *your* happiness because they want so much to be happy themselves. Therefore it's a good thing. The idea behind it is good, anyhow. The only trouble with it is that the direction is misplaced."

[2] Only five of the seventy-odd "poems" of Wolfe arranged by John S. Barnes in *A Stone, A Leaf, A Door* are taken from *You Can't Go Home Again*. The reason, however, is not only that there is less poetry in the later Wolfe, but that the poetry is less detachable. He is no longer given to deserting his characters.

rituals and routines of Mr. and Mrs. Jack, rendering the thoughts and sensations of each, give an inside view of "the world that Jack built," an intimate idea of what life in it felt like, which could not be given through George's experience.

More important, there is little sprawl in the 700-odd pages of *You Can't Go Home Again*. Aside from a few detachable scenes, such as an interesting but inconsequential chapter on a Jap who lived in George's rooming house, the novel is clearly designed and solidly constructed. Wolfe now has a firm grasp of the wealth of material that had always been at his fingertips, and had once flowed too freely. In a series of major episodes, each with its own dramatic theme, he steadily complicates, deepens and broadens his main theme—the realization that the man, the artist, the American could not go home again. The progress of the novel is a recapitulation of all the meanings of Wolfe's lifelong pilgrimage.[3]

Specifically, his theme is developed as follows. Upon returning to Libya Hill for the funeral of Aunt Maw, George Webber realizes that his homecoming is a final leavetaking; he severs the last tie to his native earth. At a brilliant party given by Esther, he says farewell to love and to his youthful dreams of the enchanted world. With the publication of his first novel, shortly after the stock

[3] Edward Aswell, it will be remembered, had to cut out extraneous material and to supply occasional continuity from the mass of manuscript deposited with him, and he was unable to follow a tentative outline that Wolfe left. But Wolfe's main design is unmistakable. No editor could have laid bare so firm a structure beneath the mass of manuscript that became *Of Time and the River*.

market crash, he is profoundly humiliated by the furious resentment of his hometown, but he also begins to realize that his personal crisis is related to the national crisis; America too had come to a crossroads. Living alone in Brooklyn during the black years of the depression, he experiences the full impact of the national catastrophe, the more keenly because of his own doubt and desperation as he concentrates on the quest of fame. During a stay in England he meets Lloyd McHarg (Sinclair Lewis), a writer who had wooed Fame and won her; and he sees that it was an empty victory—though as usual he must experience this himself before he really learns the lesson. During a stay in Germany, at the height of his own fame and happiness, he gradually realizes the terrible evil that had come into the world with Hitler, and he realizes, too, that it is akin to the desperate sickness of America; yet he feels that America is "still the New World of mankind's hope." Then he sums up everything he has learned in a farewell letter to Foxhall Edwards, his editor and friend, the father of his spirit: he can't go back to his dreams of love and art and fame, to the ivory tower or the rural retreat, to "the escapes of Time and Memory," to his foster-father—to anyone or anything that can relieve him of the burden of finding his own way in the confusion and conflict of the modern world. But he has found himself, he now knows his way; and he concludes with the statement of his belief that America too will find itself, rediscover its deathless dream. His last words are prophetic:

Dear Fox, old friend, thus we have come to the end of the road that we were to go together. My tale is finished—and so farewell.

But before I go, I have just one more thing to tell you:

Something has spoken to me in the night, burning the tapers of the waning year; something has spoken in the night, and told me I shall die, I know not where. Saying:

"To lose the earth you know, for greater knowing; to lose the life you have, for greater life; to leave the friends you loved, for greater loving; to find a land more kind than home, more large than earth—"

"—Whereon the pillars of this earth are founded, toward which the conscience of the world is tending—a wind is rising, and the rivers flow."

Thus did Wolfe live out his Faustian myth. In a sense, his spiritual development parallels that of Goethe, as reflected in the major works from the *Sorrows of Werther* to *Wilhelm Meister* to *Faust*; if his growth was more uncertain, confused and incomplete, the pattern was similar. Likewise he bears some resemblance to Thomas Mann's Joseph. Joseph had the advantage of a wise, humane creator, a creator considerably more deft and conscientious than Providence; he could live his myth with consummate, self-conscious artistry, adorning it "with all sorts of solemn flourishes and pious maneuvers," treating it with the "light touch" that its solemnity called for, knowing that "only in lightness" can the spirit of man rise above the unanswerable questions of life and death. Wolfe, having to live out his own myth, could hardly be such a smiling, assured artist; his light touch was the "strong element of satiric exaggeration" appropriate to his story of "the innocent man discovering life," and to the nature of American life; but his satire was seldom light, seldom directed at his hero, because the innocent man had a very painful time, and little sense of humor. Nevertheless Wolfe blundered along the same path that Joseph danced down.

His, too, was the "artistic ego," which in its "inexcusable egocentricity" starts with "the dangerous assumption that everybody must love it more than himself," but which also has a natural sympathy for others and thereby "finds its way into the social," identifies itself with the communal life.

This is a well-beaten path, a hackneyed story—and properly so; for the myth is quotation. "The truth is," writes Mann, "that life is a mingling of the individual elements and the formal stock-in-trade; a mingling in which the individual, as it were, only lifts his head above the formal and impersonal elements. Much that is extra-personal, much unconscious identification, much that is conventional and schematic, is none the less decisive for the experience not only of the artist but of the human being in general." The innocence of George Webber and the elementary discoveries he makes might well have been viewed more ironically, treated more playfully, but they are appropriate to Wolfe's myth. The elementary is also the elemental, and for sophisticated contemporaries it is perhaps the hardest thing to learn—as Somerset Maugham discovered.[4] Yet Wolfe's discoveries were not simply elementary. As he grew aware of the "conventional and schematic" elements in his experience, found his way into the collective life, he also grew aware of forces that were radically transforming this life. He could not "go home."

---

[4] "Goodness is the only value that seems in this world of appearances to have any claim to be an end in itself," Maugham concludes in *The Summing Up*, "ashamed" to offer so commonplace, unparadoxical a testament. "It seems I have little more to say than can be read in any copybook or heard from any pulpit. I have gone a long way round to discover what everyone knew already."

Unlike Joseph, he lived in a revolutionary world; unlike Mann, he tried to restate the timeless schema in wholly contemporary terms. On all counts, I believe, *You Can't Go Home Again* merits a detailed review.

2

Wolfe's development of his main theme is quite explicit. Indeed, it is too explicit. He talks too much, repeatedly spelling out the meanings of each episode, often in words of one syllable. For the most part they are familiar meanings, which were stated in his earlier novels; the reader picks them up long before George Webber does, and may grow impatient at his slowness. Nevertheless *You Can't Go Home Again* is much more than a bald restatement. Wolfe is consistently sober; meanings that once were chanted in ecstasy, in fury, or in despair, and that accordingly had to be discounted, may now be taken at their face value because he himself has first discounted them, on the basis of the incongruities which are the source of our ecstasy, fury and despair. Moreover, he consistently relates his personal experience to the experience of the nation, and finally to the timeless story of man's seeking and not finding. And he also dramatizes his meanings, stating them not merely in essays but in concrete terms of character and incident.

Thus George's farewell to his hometown is heralded and symbolized by Judge Bland, the most striking of Wolfe's "free creations." George meets him on the train to Libya Hill (in Pullman K-19), where he also hears some leading citizens talking feverishly about the local real estate boom.

129

A notorious usurer, the Judge is old, frail, syphilitic and blind, with the ghost of an evil, mocking smile perpetually hovering about the corners of his sunken mouth; he is lewd, horribly corrupt, "genuinely, unfathomably evil"; and he is also "enormously attractive" in his lost goodness, his secret integrity, his ironic dignity and humor. He speaks with cold contempt of the leading citizens, the pious Puritans who are in the big money and who condone his modest graft because it squeezes only a "bunch of niggers." "My dear boy," he tells George, "I assure you that I am utterly blind. I can no longer distinguish one of our most prominent local bastards two feet off.—Now, *Jarvis*," he suddenly adds, addressing the most prominent; and he proceeds to recite, in a terrible, toneless voice, the story of their corruption and hypocrisy. He also warns George: "Do you think you can really go *home* again?"

Supposedly George had thought so, even dreamed of this homecoming; though it has long been plain enough that his destiny lay in the land of his father, not of the deathless and death-haunted Joyners. At any rate, he finds Libya Hill the more depressing because it has become a boomtown. All the townspeople are madly buying and selling real estate, making millions on paper while mortgaging away their lives; all are ruining their city and themselves to build uglier, more expensive homes and country clubs, meaningless streets and bridges, shining tunnels into the mountain wilderness; and their hysterically free enterprise, their American dream of the better life, only accentuates the meagerness and joylessness of their lives. Judge Bland, George thinks, may be the key to the whole tragedy. He is shamelessly evil because something good

THE END OF THE ROAD

in him has not died; he is lost because he had sought warmth and light in this darkness, offered gifts of hope, intelligence and joy that had been rejected. He is a victim of the smugness and the sterility of provincial life.

This dispassionate social criticism that has replaced the bitter personal protests of Wolfe's early work is more pronounced in the next episode, in which George finally says farewell to Esther and her world. The dramatic means is a brilliant party given by Esther. Wolfe renders it with the exhaustiveness of Dostoyevsky, devoting almost two hundred pages to the events of a single day.

Esther now lives in a spacious, grandly simple apartment on Park Avenue. ("The amount of simplicity that could be purchased even in those times for a yearly rental of fifteen thousand dollars was quite considerable.") The guests at her party include some genuinely distinguished people in the world of finance and of the arts. They also include fashionable homosexuals, lechers, wasters and assorted decadents. The highlight of the evening is an entertainment provided by "Piggy Logan" and his circus of wire dolls; Mr. Logan's circus was the rage at a time when it was smart to be supercilious about great writers of the past, and ecstatic about the great art of comic strips, Charlie Chaplin and Broadway entertainers. But the distinguished and the decadent are alike in their complacent acceptance of their privileged world. They are very sure of themselves even though they have little faith, very pleased with themselves even though they are often bored —and it was also fashionable to be bored by many things. At best they are like Lawrence Hirsch, a great captain of finance and industry. He is a patron of the arts, enlightened, humane and wise; he is celebrated for his liberal views on child labor, share-cropping, Russia and the Sacco-Vanzetti case; yet his wealth as a banker ultimately comes from the exploitation of the many with whom he sincerely sympathizes—outside the hours when business is business. He too accepts a society honeycombed with privilege, self-interest and dishonesty.

George Webber, however, suddenly sees that he must break with it—or lose his soul as an artist. This fabulous world is "the deadliest enemy of art and truth." It has corrupted many writers, driven others to seek refuge in "forlorn and esoteric little cults and isms." George cannot sing America if he is saddled with the "stultifying burden" of privilege. It all came down to this:

In America, of all places, there could be no honest compromise with special privilege. Privilege and truth could not lie down together. He thought of how a silver dollar, if held close enough to the eye, could blot out the sun itself. There were stronger, deeper tides and currents running in America than any which these glamorous lives tonight had ever plumbed or even dreamed of. Those were the depths that he would like to sound.

George is exhilarated as his confusion is resolved in this clear vision, and complications become simple.

They become, perhaps, a bit too simple. One may sense an *ex post facto* element in Wolfe's rationalization of his break with Esther; one may add that he himself continued to lead a relatively privileged life, and to enjoy the company of other privileged people whose incomes had capitalistic sources; one may doubt that his occasional attendance at such parties as Esther's was a serious threat to his sincerity or his truth; one may suspect that his desire for personal freedom was stronger than his fear of silver dollars blotting out his sun. There are also lingering traces of his provincial jealousy and resentment, as when he pictures Mr. Jack anticipating the "brilliant gayety" of his wife's party, with "some yokel, say, fresh from the rural districts, all hands and legs and awkwardness, hooked and wriggling on a cruel and cunning word." The whole affair seems somewhat less significant than Wolfe's exhaustive account of it implies it is. After the first flush of his exhilaration, George is wearied, saddened, desolated by a sense of loss, as he at last gives up the glorious dreams of his youth; but the readers may also be wearied by this protracted farewell to a world that Wolfe had been satirizing ever since *Of Time and the River*.

Yet his account is essentially just. Wolfe no longer rants about Esther, the Jews, the city-bred, or any other mortal enemies; neither does he assert his immortal privilege and passion as an artist. He is stressing very real and glaring social inequalities, which an American artist may not be obliged to condemn in order to preserve his integrity, but which are unquestionably a central issue of American life, and one that cannot be ignored by an artist aspiring to write a comprehensive American myth. The satiric exaggeration in his account is also artistically appropriate. For Esther's party marks the end of an era: it is held in the autumn of 1929, exactly a week before the stock market crash.

Symbolically, her brilliantly staged affair ends with an unscheduled climax. A fire breaks out in the apartment house; presently all the lights go out; tenants and guests mill around in the great central courtyard, in helpless confusion. "For in the well-ordered world in which these people lived, something had gone suddenly wrong. Things had got out of control. They were the lords and masters of the earth, vested with authority and accustomed to command, but now the control had been taken from them." None of the wealthy tenants are injured, however. The only casualties are two menials, elevator men who were trapped in stalled elevators and suffocated by smoke. Nobody knows about this except the police and a hard-boiled reporter; the management wants to keep it quiet. The Jacks return to their apartment, where "everything seemed curiously unchanged"; though a sudden tremor in the building recalls to Esther a rumor she had heard that evening about faint tremors in the stock market. In a few days comes the crash that no management can keep quiet. Everything is changed.

The leaders of the nation try to go home again; home is just around the corner, and is fundamentally sound. So Wolfe now broadens his refrain: America, too, can't go home again. It had come to the end of something, and to the beginning of something else. Although no one knew what that something else would be, and many grew desperate in their uncertainty and insecurity, Wolfe begins to sound his faith: the real America, the America that had always been, was now emerging from its imprisonment, stunned, blinded, but "full of latent vitality." Similarly with George Webber. Not only is he as confused and fearful as everybody else, but the publication of his first novel, shortly after the crash, marks an end and a beginning for him—the end of his obscurity and the beginning of new trials.

He is quickly disillusioned by the lion hunters. But he is increasingly distressed, ashamed, appalled by the flood of violently abusive letters from his hometown. Here Wolfe is again recording his own experience literally. He still defends himself too warmly against the charge of autobiography and against the praise of his wonderful memory. He describes his novel rather inaccurately as a "*Ulysses* kind of book"—an acknowledgment of his debt to Joyce in which he at once flatters himself too much and undervalues his native genius. On the whole, however, he now gives a judicious appraisal of *Look Homeward, Angel*.

Fairly enough, Wolfe attributes the furious resentment of the townspeople in part to "something wounded" in the South, the secret fears, shames, lusts and sorrows that were repressed beneath the outward forms of their proud mythology and bigot theology, and that were intensified by the hurt and the hypocrisy of all America. Southern writers had never told them the truth about themselves. Chiefly, however, Wolfe emphasizes that he himself had not succeeded in telling the truth. There was truth in the book, but it was distorted by "his vanity, egotism, hot passion, and lacerated pride," which had nothing to do with art or his integrity. Hence his hero was "a stick, a fool, a prig, a snob"; his whole vision, though "accurate and Joycean" within particular frames, was "false, mannered, and untrue" in a larger frame. Wolfe is somewhat excessive, indeed, in this self-criticism, as if his pride were still lacerated. He introduces Randy Shepperton, a friend from Libya Hill, to carry on a long, stilted argument with George. In his anguish George tries to play the martyr, the "wounded faun," reverting to Ganty talk about the Artist

135

who lives on beauty and truth and is thereby doomed to be a social outcast; whereupon Randy makes him squirm some more.

In any event, Wolfe stresses that business also had its wounded fauns, business was "the most precious form of egotism." The hard-headed, practical businessmen—"the real rulers of America"—were completely wrong about the depression from the start. And Randy himself—the clear-eyed Randy who is nobody's fool—is a symbol of this American tragedy. In Libya Hill the collapse of the boom was complete and spectacular, beginning with the suicide of the mayor. Randy has lost his job but is optimistic; a good salesman can always find a job. He even rejoices in his feeling of freedom. Before long, however, he is frantic in his freedom. He cannot find a job, uses up his savings, and is forced to sell the family home. Finally he goes on relief. He has found that he can't go back to the super-colossal salesman's paradise that he had thought was America. Nobody's fool, he had been fooled by the whole order, the "American way of life."

The ruin of Randy, of Libya Hill, of the South, of America meant much more, Wolfe insists, than the breakdown of the "capitalist system." The deeper ruin, the essence of the catastrophe, was moral, intellectual, spiritual. The values by which Americans had been living were false; it was the hollowness of their lives that had made possible all the noise and bustle. Hence many rugged individualists were committing suicide—they had to kill themselves because they had no real self apart from the lost symbols of their prosperity, or because they realized that they had died long ago. Many more still had faith only because they

136

lacked the intellectual honesty and courage to face themselves. But whence this national corruption? "It seems to me," George tells Randy (and here he seems to have read Vernon Parrington), "that America went off the track somewhere—back around the time of the Civil War." It had taken to the way of easy wealth and graft, special pleading for special privilege, in which self-interest was 99.44% pure and wore a schoolgirl complexion and four out of five had it. "And the real things like freedom, and equal opportunity, and the integrity and worth of the individual—things that have belonged to the American dream since the beginning—they have become just words, too."

Just why America went off the track Wolfe does not say. Had he concerned himself with this pertinent question he might have been less casual in his reference to the capitalist system. Possibly, too, he would have been less insistent in his ridicule of the literary and intellectual communists, a rather unpleasant ridicule that grows tiresome. The objects of his satire, however, were in fact much more tiresome and unpleasant. In justice if not in charity, one must recall the solemn silliness and earnest savagery of this period in our letters, when critics and professors could prove that they were Comrades only by slaughtering "bourgeois" writers, writers whose "social consciousness" was not utter or utterly orthodox. Wolfe was among their victims. Nevertheless no other American novelist has left a more comprehensive, searching report of the depression era. The "proletarian" writers documented more thoroughly the plight of the unemployed, but for all their sincerity and their intensity, their novels were generally crude, narrow

137

and artistically superficial; already the bulk of this fiction is dead, or of interest only as historical document. Wolfe tried to view the calamity in a larger perspective, against the background of the history and the destiny of the nation. If he did not emphasize the economic and political causes of the calamity, he was not blind or indifferent to them. He chose to dwell on the more immediate human consequences, the meanings in terms of personal hopes, fears and aspirations, which are apt to be˙overlooked by economic and political theorists (though not by politicians), which he knew directly from his own observation and felt experience, which are the natural subject matter of imaginative literature, and which are also the ultimate meanings, the presumed ends of political programs.

From this point of view, a more legitimate criticism of Wolfe's rendering of the national catastrophe is his failure to dramatize it in the experience of any important character. (Randy Shepperton's unhappy story is merely summarized in a page.) Chiefly he presents it at second hand, through the observation and reflection of George Webber. George (like Wolfe) quits teaching to give all his time to his second novel, and for four years deliberately holes up in Brooklyn, in the most isolated, forlorn hiding place he can find—a basement apartment near the old Gowanus canal. Having had his little taste of glory, and of ashes, he now concentrates desperately on a quest of fame, in the belief that the reason for the ashy taste was that he had not been good enough. His next novel must prove that he is no seven-day wonder. But his desperation is heightened by his nightly prowlings about New York, in which he constantly sees the terrible ravages of the depression. The symbol is the public latrine in front of the New York City Hall, where homeless, hopeless men spend the night, sometimes fighting savagely for possession of the stools. The derelicts include perennial stumblebums, but most of them are victims of the general ruin: "honest, decent, middle-aged men with faces seamed by toil and want," young men drifting over the nation in search of work or crumbs—the uprooted, unwanted, dispensable men of America. And only a few blocks away, by brutal contrast, the pinnacles of Wall Street soar above the mighty vaults where much of the world's wealth is locked away.

Such scenes, however, are supplemented by scenes of "normal" American life: men hanging around the corners of shabby Brooklyn streets in the month of March, dressed in their cheap "good" Sunday clothes, waiting interminably for nothing at all—yet always confident that something is sure to happen, something is bound to turn up. To stress the blight of industrialism, Wolfe does create a dramatic symbol, out of a routine newspaper story. It is "an unidentified man" who registered at the Admiral Francis Drake Hotel as C. Green and then "fell or jumped" to his death from the twelfth story—a cipher exploded on the pavement of Brooklyn. To C. Green, Wolfe devotes a striking chapter.

He is one of the "hollow men," meager of mind and dull of sense, empty of juice or salt, used to grinding traffic, swarming pavements, the "concrete horrors" of blazing noons, the "tormented hodgepodge of our architectures," the tawdry splendors of advertising signs. He is no man like Francis Drake. The lusty Admiral Drake could never even have imagined C. Green, hurtling down concrete

139

roads on Sunday with a million other ciphers, at night prowling over a mug of coffee and a tabloid at Joe the Greek's. Now the remains of C. Green are spattered on an American sidewalk: the "most impersonal pavement in the world," the "cement Mobway" built by the "Standard Concentrated Production Units of America." It is no real street, no place to amble, but a channel, a "kind of tube for a projectile, a kind of groove for millions and millions of projectiles, all driven past incessantly, all beetling onward, bearing briefly white slugged blurs of driven flesh." It is one of the ten thousand "arteries" of Brooklyn, "Standard Concentrated Chaos No. 1," triumphant "Standard Concentrated Blot upon the Face of the Earth." In short, Wolfe's satire becomes pretty labored—to the end of his career he was never content to say a thing once, and rarely content to leave a meaning implicit. But it is not simply bitter. It is colored by pity, and finally touched by respect. C. Green—"Poor little guy!"—came to life by killing himself. Just "another guy," he became "*the* guy"; he identified "a single spot of all our general Nothingness with the unique passion, the awful terror, and the dignity of Death." The brave Admiral, Wolfe concludes, must not be too sure that we are the hollow men.

In the immediate context, this conclusion may seem merely ironical, or forced; and it is not wholly convincing from any point of view. (This chapter was written several years before the rest of the story was completed.) But the context is widened as George finally comes out of the wilderness of Brooklyn and again goes abroad to work. In England he gets a different perspective on America through Mrs. Purvis, his charwoman. She is a model servant, devoted to the point of slavishness; she worries about the nobility, poor things, and becomes pink with indignation when she reads that some duke has to sell one of his estates because of high taxes; she worships the Prince of Wales; she is also extravagantly fond of animals, and extravagantly indignant at the slightest mistreatment of them; and she has no feeling whatever for a half-starved, half-naked, wholly wretched little delivery boy, one of the gnomish race of Little People. Poverty in England is more degraded than any George had known in America—but to Mrs. Purvis it is as natural and inevitable as the fog, and as pointless to protest against. The idea that anything could or should be done about the sufferings of the poor never enters her head.

In England George also meets the world-famous Lloyd McHarg, who had just received the greatest literary honor the world has to offer, and in his speech of acceptance had hailed George as a man of genius, a pledge of America's promise.[5] McHarg tells him to write another big, fat novel with lots of people in it, and not to worry about the criticism of the bright young men. "Take all the instruction you can absorb. But remember that no amount of instruction can ever take the place of the wallop in the old right hand." More important, McHarg discourages George by his living example of the hollowness of fame. One of "the

[5] The reference is to Sinclair Lewis's speech on receiving the Nobel prize. Wolfe's expression of gratitude here is touchingly unaffected and unreserved. He also repays the compliment, however, by one of his most vivid portraits. His Lloyd McHarg is a characteristic bundle of incongruities, which are heightened as usual by "satiric exaggeration"; but his picture is drawn with more warmth and affection than usual.

141

truly great people of the world," who reminds George of Lincoln in his astonishing ugliness and his enormous dignity, he is now warm, lusty and generous, now feverish, irritable and harsh, torn between an insatiable hunger for "the world of natural humanity" and an incurable disgust with its natural representatives.

One of these is his traveling companion, a florid, shrewd, smug businessman from Holland. Through this Dutch Babbitt, George discovers that small businessmen are a race, a universal and not merely an American type. (Although George is now seeing things in relation and in perspective, no longer overwhelmed by "Amount and Number," he is perhaps unduly excited by such "astonishing" discoveries of "identities of concept and of essence" beneath surface differences.) In another friend of McHarg's, a charming English gentleman-writer, he discovers the race of futilitarians, the hollow men of the arts. Unequal to the conditions of modern life, unable to find belief or bottom in the world because he has none in himself, this man has retreated to a charming rural estate where he writes books expressing his "illusioned disillusion." His American fellow half-men were to be found in Boston salons, Paris cafés, little Bohemias, or New England farms where they lived an elaborately simple life, cultivating the soil and a self-conscious love of "the earth."

The climax of this indirect revelation of America comes in George's visit to Germany, after the publication of his second novel has made him famous. Germany had always been for him an enchanted land, in which he felt more at home than any other except America. The Germans are now lionizing him as the "American Homer," appreciating his epic intentions even more than his countrymen do; everywhere he is warmed by the admiration of cultured men and the adoration of lovely women; he is the lord of the earth, with a confidence, a sense of power, a radiant gladness and affection such as he had never known. Then, little by little, the poison of Nazi Germany seeps in. A fleeting look of terror, a sudden malignancy as swiftly concealed, a desperate pleading of an eye, in time a guarded disclosure behind shuttered windows in the midnight watches, and finally a flood of confessions of hatred and despair make George aware that an entire nation is mortally ill.[6] The malady is a ubiquitous fear that has twisted and blighted all human relations. It is an evil far deeper and more sinister than the harsh corruption and naked violence of American business and public life. George realizes the full horror of it as he takes leave of Germany. A fellow passenger in his train compartment—a very fussy, fidgety, ill-tempered little man who had gradually warmed up to his companions—is arrested at the border. He is a Jew trying to escape the country. George sees him on the platform, white-faced, greasy with sweat, "protesting vol-

[6] Franz Schoenberner, editor of the pre-Nazi magazine *Simplicissimus,* has paid tribute to Wolfe's "almost terrifying clairvoyance," declaring that in these fewer than a hundred pages Wolfe gave "a deeper insight into the much-discussed 'German problem' than all the endless cables and reports of all the legions of American correspondents combined." Another measure of Wolfe's growing social consciousness, incidentally, is provided by the first reference to Nazi Germany in his letters to his mother. Hitler unfortunately came into power about the time *Look Homeward, Angel* was published in Germany. Wolfe expresses concern because he does not know whether "this trouble which they are having there now has hurt its sale or not."

143

ubly in a voice that had a kind of anguished lilt," smiling a "horrible little forced smile of terror" that is more horrible because of the intolerable slow smile of his guards. George sees him again as the train leaves for France:

And the little man—he, too, paused once from his feverish effort to explain. As the car in which he had been riding slid by, he lifted his pasty face and terror-stricken eyes, and for a moment his lips were stilled of their anxious pleading. He looked once, directly and steadfastly, at his former companions, and they at him. And in that gaze there was all the unmeasured weight of man's mortal anguish. George and the others felt somehow naked and ashamed, and somehow guilty. They all felt that they were saying farewell, not to a man, but to humanity; not to some pathetic stranger, some chance acquaintance of the voyage, but to mankind; not to some nameless cipher out of life, but to the fading image of a brother's face.

In this corruption of a great people George sees a great tragedy, and no reason for simple hatred. He also sees an ancient and universal evil, not simply a modern or German perversion. It is the Dark Ages come again, "shocking beyond belief, but true as the hell that man forever creates for himself"; it is a savagery old as Time, the heritage of the whole race, which has always been the enemy of man. Hence George sees that the same primitive spirit of greed, lust and ruthless force is alive in America. Memories of all he had seen in Brooklyn come flooding back, but now they form an integrated picture: the evil of haggard, homeless men seeking food in garbage cans, shelter in foul latrines, while the glittering upperworld remains coldly indifferent to the misery and injustice on which its life is founded, is related to the evil in Germany, and to the whole history of man's inhumanity to man. For the first time George real-

144

izes how desperately sick America is. Yet he is glad to come back home. In America there is "still air to breathe in, and winds to clear the air"; its sickness is not incurable, its promise has not been utterly shattered. Wolfe reaffirms one of the main articles of the American faith expressed by countless writers and orators before him—the Mission of America:

America was young, America was still the New World of mankind's hope, America was not like this old and worn-out Europe which seethed and festered with a thousand deep and uncorrected ancient maladies. America was still resilient, still responsive to a cure—if only—if only—men could somehow cease to be afraid of truth.

The quotation is from the thirty-seven page farewell letter to Foxhall Edwards that sums up and concludes the novel. This amounts to an autobiographical essay, and it is not, I should say at once, an artistically logical or effective ending. In part it is needless repetition; Wolfe restates the basic meanings of the novel, making them still more explicit but not much more meaningful. For the rest the letter is a personal postscript, very interesting to students of his career, but undramatic and loosely joined to the supposed life of George Webber. Wolfe almost forgets the pretense that it is George who is writing the letter. Thus he mentions for the first time a tragic incident that led to George's expulsion from college and his disenfranchisement: he had been involved in a hazing which ended in accidental death.[7] Adding that he was soon pardoned,

[7] John Terry informs me that Wolfe himself was not involved in this incident, which occurred several years before his time.

THOMAS WOLFE

Wolfe insists that he was not warped by this painful affair. "It is vitally important to me," he writes, "to make one thing clear: that I am not the victim or the embittered martyr of anything that ever happened in the past." It was indeed vitally important to Wolfe himself to refute such unflattering explanations of the "bitterness" of his early novels; but his confession is a superfluous footnote to the biography of George Webber, whose career has already been explained.

Moreover, the fictional excuse for the letter is unconvincing, even though the occasion is not fictitious. George Webber is explaining to Foxhall Edwards, his friend and the father of his youth—in other words, Wolfe is explaining to Maxwell Perkins—why they have reached the parting of the ways, and why the end of their ideal relationship is as inevitable as was its beginning. This would seem to be a momentous decision, a turning point; for Wolfe has made much of the father symbol all through his legend. The trouble, however, is that he failed to dramatize this relationship. At the beginning of *You Can't Go Home Again* we are told briefly that in Fox Edwards, George found the father he had been looking for; during the Brooklyn years we are told that he went to his foster-father whenever he was overwhelmed by desolation and doubt, and always had his power and belief wonderfully restored; at the end we read a moving tribute to the tireless, selfless loyalty of his editor, which had carried him through nine years of turmoil. But we are merely told—we are never shown. Although Wolfe paints a vivid picture of Fox Edwards at home, in one of his characteristic early morning scenes, he presents no scenes at all between Fox and

146

George. Similarly he fails to dramatize the parting itself, or to show how and why it became "inevitable."

In effect, then, the final chapters of *You Can't Go Home Again* are addressed directly to Maxwell Perkins, and through him to Wolfe's critics, to his fellow-Americans and to posterity. They constitute quite literally his final testament. And since they are so personal, we may raise a personal question. Wolfe declares, convincingly, that George Webber is no longer lost, no longer needs a foster-father; but this does not explain why he must part with his editor and friend. The declared reason—an essential difference in their philosophies—would not seem to make the separation necessary, much less inevitable. One actual reason was simple embarrassment: Wolfe had reached the stage in his narrative where he had to deal with his relations with Perkins and Scribner's. Another was the sting of criticism—the charges of Bernard DeVoto in particular had rankled. Perhaps most important was a need of proving to himself that he could write novels by himself, but even in this healthy desire for independence we may suspect some jealous resentment of his former dependence, some fear of any close bonds; or in other words Wolfe was actually somewhat less independent, and more egotistical, than he thought. Love and Fame were not enough—nothing can be enough, except perhaps the deep, close, continuous personal relationships that he was unable to maintain. A measure of personal inadequacy is suggested by his more evident love of America than of Americans, his too evident fondness for satiric exaggeration, the touch of acerbity or malice in even his affectionate portraits, as of Lloyd McHarg and Foxhall Edwards. The one important character

147

he treats with entire affection, and without satiric exaggeration, is Nebraska Crane—who is a pure invention, born of wish-fulfillment.

Nevertheless such observations lead to a more important observation. Wolfe's private problems no longer seriously cloud or distort his vision of larger relationships, in particular those of the artist to the group and the age. He has in fact come to satisfactory terms with his society, terms recognizing not merely the desirability of "cooperation" but the fact of kinship. His disagreement with his editor is at least the means to a clear, full realization of the faith he ended with, the meanings that give his personal legend the wider reference and deeper vitality of the myth.

Foxhall Edwards, according to Wolfe, is Ecclesiastes.[8] He is always gentle, patient and kind; whatever his hand finds to do he does with all his might, performing prodigies of devoted effort; and his main effort is to help others who are wasting their might, to save all that is worth saving and can be saved. At the same time he is fatally resigned—convinced that the evil that is, has always been and will always be, because it is the primary condition of man's being, and that there is no new thing under the sun, save perhaps the new monsters which replace the old. Wolfe also begins with Ecclesiastes. He is no less aware of the ancient monsters lurking in the dark unconscious, the genuine evil in the spirit of man. Yet he does not end with Ecclesiastes:

In everlasting terms—those of eternity—you and the Preacher may be right: for there is no greater wisdom than the wisdom of

[8] Maxwell Perkins disclaims this exalted kinship. He declares that he deliberately talked like Ecclesiastes because he thought that it would do Wolfe good.

148

Ecclesiastes, no acceptance finally so true as the stern fatalism of the rock. Man was born to live, to suffer, and to die, and what befalls him is a tragic lot. There is no denying this in the final end. *But we must, dear Fox, deny it all along the way.*

Whatever the fate of Man, men must combat the ancient evil, in the faith that it can be conquered and destroyed. To accept it as inevitable and irremediable is to make it so.

Specifically, Wolfe ends with his American credo: "I believe that we are lost here in America, but I believe we shall be found." He adds that this belief is not only his own hope but "America's everlasting, living dream." The everlasting enemy has also been with us from the beginning. He is "single selfishness and compulsive greed"; he is blind, but has "the brutal power of his blind grab." No blind optimism can withstand this power. Truth alone can resist it—the "plain and searching light of truth" that in Germany had been extinguished. Americans must lose their fear of truth, and their fear of looking in the face of fear. Wolfe goes further and hints of the "radicalism" for which his editor had half seriously reproached him: the conquest of the enemy will demand "nothing less than the complete revision of the structure of society as we know it." But in the face of this formidable task he reasserts his faith:

> I think the true discovery of America is before us. I think the true fulfillment of our spirit, of our people, of our mighty and immortal land, is yet to come. I think the true discovery of our own democracy is still before us. And I think that all these things are certain as the morning, as inevitable as noon.

The inevitability of this happy outcome is open to considerable question, on Wolfe's own terms. Since he wrote,

149

Americans have had the benefit of another world war, in which the enemy was again defeated; but truth still seems not too popular, fear is still strong, the enemy is still with us. Now we have atomic power, with its incalculable possibilities which at their worst can be calculated all too readily. As Spengler prophetically wrote, we are no longer at liberty to hope what we please about the future, but must inform ourselves of what can happen, and what will happen. As for Wolfe, to repeat, it is doubtful that he had informed himself of all the economic and political implications of his casual remark about the revision of our society. Yet the event has not made his testament obsolete. If the danger is far graver today, it arises still more plainly from "single selfishness and compulsive greed"; if survival calls for a high degree of political intelligence, it also calls for courage, honesty, good will—the moral values that Wolfe stressed. His faith, which at bottom is an animal faith, an assumption necessary for our living purposes and implicit in the purposiveness even of those who insist that it is an impossible conclusion, is also a genuinely philosophical faith.

As a self-conscious satirist—and butt—of "intellectuals," Wolfe was at pains to disavow the youthful passion for "concepts" that earned him a One in his philosophy courses in college (which was also his way of suggesting that he could handle concepts as well as the intellectuals if he cared to). He turned down an invitation to contribute to *Modern-Day Philosophies*, he tells Fox Edwards, because he was unwilling to say that he had such a philosophy, unready to commit his belief to formal, final concepts. "The essence of Time is Flow, not Fix." Because growth, change, is the essential reality, question and doubt are essential to belief; unless a man's philosophy flows and grows with him, "his body of beliefs is nothing but a series of fixations." Nevertheless Wolfe is here stating a philosophy, and a "modern-day" one. It is substantially the philosophy of John Dewey, with his emphasis upon Becoming instead of Being, constant inquiry instead of absolute knowledge, truths instead of the Truth.[9] It is in line with the current scientific conception of a creative, evolving universe in which reality itself is on the make, and there are new things under the sun. If Wolfe is rationalizing a very personal sense of life, stressing Flow because of his extraordinarily keen senses and retentive memory, stressing Growth because it was so peculiarly the form and meaning of his own life, he is being true to his native genius and to his deepest experience. And if this philosophy provides no guarantees, if it makes ultimate uncertainty a fundamental principle, by the same token it provides grounds for hope; for man may literally *make* the best of his world, or at least make for better.

Critics still tend to discount or even disregard Wolfe's testament, as either a desperate act of faith or a mere afterthought. "It is clear," wrote the implacable Bernard De-Voto in 1940, "that Wolfe could never have overcome the forces of disintegration; they had already defeated him." But even the temperate Alfred Kazin writes that *You Can't Go Home Again* is "rooted in a conviction of decline and

[9] "The moment philosophy supposes it can become a final and comprehensive solution," Dewey writes in his *Logic: The Theory of Inquiry*, "it ceases to be inquiry and becomes either apologetics or propaganda."

fall, of emptiness and dissolution." He links Wolfe with Faulkner, as the extreme symbols of "a perpetual mal du siècle, a furious sickness and rage"; they are "the epic recorders of demoralization and collapse, specialists in doom." He makes Wolfe perhaps the clearest illustration of his main thesis in *On Native Grounds:* the "deep and subtle alienation," the "terrible estrangement" of American writers from the American world they are absorbed in. And so here is the final issue of Wolfe's work, as of modern literature generally. There is no mistaking what Wolfe says—he had announced that *You Can't Go Home Again* was to be "a book . . . of discovery, hence of union with life," and at the end explicitly affirms the union. The only question is whether he really knew all that he said, thoroughly felt it, thoroughly believed it. I believe that he had indeed made his peace, with his world and with himself.

The immediate evidence is the quiet tone of his credo. If Wolfe is careless and inconsistent in declaring the realization of the American dream "inevitable," he otherwise writes in a low pitch. There is nothing shrill, no hint of desperation or panic; neither is there any verbal ecstasy, any celebration induced by the power, or the habit, of his own language. This impression of mental health is confirmed, moreover, by his notes on "A Western Journey," a diary of a long automobile trip he took through the Far West a few months before his death. These hurried jottings reveal his lifelong passion to be "writing it all up," as well as some traces of his youthful passion for Amount and Number. ("And 535 miles today!") But they also reveal his gusto, his eagerness to learn still more about America, his pleasure in the natural wonders of the land and in "people, people, people"—even in the tinsel joys and loves of the vacationing stenographers, shopgirls and schoolteachers. There is little suggestion here of "demoralization" or "estrangement," much less of any "furious sickness and rage." [10]

The essential proof of Wolfe's credo, however, must lie in his novels—in the concrete representation of the thought and feeling by which he earned his faith. "Never trust the artist," wrote D. H. Lawrence; "trust the story." And this study has failed of its main purpose if it has not demonstrated that Wolfe did thoroughly earn his faith, and earn it in the way of the tragic poets, by going through the worst possibilities of life. In *You Can't Go Home Again* this development can hardly be missed, for it is the explicit theme of the book; though I should emphasize that George Webber's successive disillusionments are also a gradual discovery of deeper sources of strength and wisdom that he *can* go home to. In the early novels the development is erratic, uncertain, confused by the many fierce revulsions, but it is apparent in retrospect; Eugene Gant, the self-centered romantic, begins to discover the elementary facts of social life even though he does not really learn them. Growth is quite literally the theme and pattern of Wolfe's

[10] I should add a personal testimony, based on a few days I spent with Wolfe immediately after he left New York for the West. Although at times he talked somberly of the idea that he couldn't go home again, he never seemed like a man torn by uncertainty, haunted by thoughts of doom, or obsessed by any desperate emotion. He was obviously happy in the work he had just completed; for the most part he was boyishly exuberant, delighting in a new landscape, in simple talk, and in such simple pleasures as a visit to a zoo or the prospect of his first ride on a streamlined train.

153

whole work, as it is with no other contemporary writer
(and with few less than with Faulkner). The outcome of
this growth was by no means inevitable. He might have
ended, as he began, in revulsion; he might have come out
of his frenzied confusion into some religious or political
absolutism, some factitious certainty. Nevertheless the actual outcome was a logical culmination, of an organic
growth; for his faith in the promise of America, and in the
dignity of man, is implicit in his earliest work. From the
very beginning he had the tragic sense of life, as well as
the passionate love of life that often goes with it, in which
humanistic values are most deeply rooted.

A fitting last word is Wolfe's last letter, written to Maxwell Perkins a few weeks before he died. It is an example
of his unstudied eloquence, which may not lend itself to
fine analysis but which can speak for itself:

Dear Max:

I'm sneaking this against orders—but "I've got a hunch"—and I
wanted to write these words to you.

I've made a long voyage and been to a strange country, and
I've seen the dark man very close; and I don't think I was too
much afraid of him, but so much of mortality still clings to me—
I wanted most desperately to live and still do, and I thought about
you all a 1000 times, and wanted to see you all again, and there
was the impossible anguish and regret of all the work I had not
done, of all the work I had to do—and I know now I'm just a
grain of dust, and I feel as if a great window has been opened on
life I did not know about before—and if I come through this, I
hope to God I am a deeper and a wise one— If I get on my feet
and out of here, it will be months before I head back, but if I get
on my feet I'll come back.

—Whatever happens—I had this "hunch" and wanted to write
you and tell you, no matter what happens or has happened, I

154

shall always think of you and feel about you the way it was that 4th of July day 3 yrs. ago when you met me at the boat, and we went out on the cafe on the river and had a drink and later went on top of the tall building and all the strangeness and the glory and the power of life and of the city way below—

Yours always

Tom

3

The manuscript that Wolfe turned over to his editor before his death contained not only his last "novels" but all his unpublished writing—material left over from his first novels, early drafts of sections later rewritten, experimental pieces, miscellaneous fragments.[11] Edward Aswell writes that Wolfe wanted him to be familiar with all of it so that they might better decide what really belonged in "the book." After Aswell extracted *The Web and the Rock* and *You Can't Go Home Again* there was still enough material to fill several more books, and from this he salvaged a final volume, *The Hills Beyond,* to which he added his illuminating personal note on Wolfe. Most important of these selected pieces is the title piece, a 150-page fragment of a novel on George Webber's maternal ancestors. Wolfe had long planned such a novel, under the title of *The Hills Beyond Pentland,* and had begun to write it years before; but Eliza Gant and Aunt Maw had kept nibbling away at this material until they used it all up. Upon finishing the story of George himself, he accordingly started afresh to provide his hero with ancestors. What he left is the family history down to about 1880, or twenty years before

[11] It is in the possession of William B. Wisdom but not yet available to students.

George's birth; completed, the novel would have ended where *The Web and the Rock* begins. This fragment is especially interesting because it is Wolfe's last work. He was writing and rewriting it shortly before he died.

This is unquestionably Wolfe's most "objective" fiction, impersonal even by high critical standards. With one or two exceptions, his characters are inventions; he is not himself the hero, nor does he identify himself with any one character; and though he comments freely on the narrative, he comments as the omniscient, dispassionate author. Likewise his style is modest and quiet. His setting is Zebulon, the wild mountain country of Old Catawba, but no demented winds go howling over the hills, nothing demoniacal haunts the savage wilderness. His characters are lusty, uninhibited backwoodsmen, but neither do they howl, snarl, or yell. In short, Wolfe is no longer possessed, but in full possession of his materials and his powers.

Hence I regret the necessity of repeating that these materials and powers are considerably less impressive than those he once struggled to control. *The Hills Beyond* is a respectable professional performance that will interest many readers but excite few, if any; I doubt that the most ardent lovers of Wolfe can find in it signs of genius, for to them in particular it is apt to seem simply dispirited. "As for Theodore," Wolfe writes of one of his Joyner clan, "well—we'll try to do our best in the pages of this book, but we know full well beforehand that it won't be good enough for Theodore. No book, no single pen, could ever do for Theodore what should be done for him." Once Wolfe would have done it—or overdone it—without this ladylike apology. As it is, he does fairly well by Theodore.

His characterization is generally sharp and vivid, especially because his dialogue is often rich. Nor is he actually dispirited. If his style is too often restrained to the point of prosiness, he nevertheless has an evident relish for his folk materials, even too obvious a relish for their picturesqueness—some of the local color is laid on with a trowel. In any event, the merits of the novel are on the surface. There is only occasional suggestion of latent depths of thought and feeling, powers in reserve. Wolfe's restraint here is seldom impressive because he does not seem to be restraining much.

From all this we are not forced to conclude that Wolfe had shot his bolt. Novelists in general do not write consistently at the top of their powers; Wolfe in particular was still growing, still experimenting. Neither can we take it for granted, however, that his best work lay before him when he died. Nothing in his later work is as good as the family scenes in *Look Homeward, Angel;* his gain in maturity was not yet a clear promise of greater American novels, and this real gain had also meant a real loss in lyric and dramatic power. What most plainly lay before him was the crucial test of the independence he declared in casting out Eugene Gant, the self-possession he claimed in cutting loose from Maxwell Perkins. For with the completion of *The Hills Beyond* he would have completed the story of George Webber. Having brought his autobiography up to date, he could not have gone on with it unless his novels were to be only a running journal of his life—"My Day" in annual installments. And though conceivably he might have done just this, with the world war as the stage for a fresh series of discoveries, his evident

157

inclination was to exercise his inventive powers and make a fresh start. He talked to Edward Aswell of a book about doctors, of another about lawyers. In particular he talked of a book about sex—he practically wrote the book, indeed, in five or six hours of excited talk one night. He was excited by Judge Woolsey's decision lifting the ban on *Ulysses;* for in his life story he had deliberately omitted much of his love life, in the hope of being able to write freely and fully about the subject later. I have misgivings about how this book might have turned out. But we cannot say with assurance in what direction he would have gone, or how far his powers could have taken him.

At least there are no hints of new directions in this final volume. *The Hills Beyond* itself not only covers ground that Wolfe had previously explored but naturally introduces much the same themes as in the novels it was designed to preface. The sturdy backwoodsmen are also prone to the romantic self-deception of the South. They too have been corrupted by compulsive greed; already Old Catawba has been sucked and gutted, its majestic hills left detimbered, eroded, scarred by empty mica pits and the dump heaps of deserted mines. Nevertheless the life of the hills folk is "increate with myth." Wolfe revels in the tall stories and bawdy legends of native heroes, who at once created the folk and were created by them; and he insists that "the Myth is true." He points to the incongruities of backwoods America as of urban America.

Likewise the shorter pieces in the volume contain familiar materials. Perhaps the best of them, a monologue called "Chickamauga" in which a Confederate veteran pours out his memories of the Civil War, belongs in the Pentland-

Joyner cycle; Wolfe got the story from one of his maternal great-uncles, and told it in the old man's words. Several other sketches are relics of Wolfe's immaturity, and it might have been more pious to have left them unpublished. "On Leprechauns," for example, is a bitter, labored satire on the deference shown foreign writers, while "the usual reception of our young native artist . . . is a good, swift kick in the teeth"; it is untrue as well as unamusing. Still another sketch, "The Lost Boy," is at first glance an interesting experiment in technique. It presents young Grover Gant (Ben's twin, and in real life Grover Wolfe) as he seemed to himself, to his mother Eliza, to his sister Helen, and to Wolfe when revisiting the scene of his death years later; Edward Aswell notes that Wolfe here tries "to extract the whole substance of an experience by getting at it on four levels at once." But though it is a touching story, its texture is not actually so subtle or so complex. Grover looks essentially the same in all four views; we get not four levels but four characters on one level. Wolfe never handled point of view with anything like the subtlety of Henry James or Conrad, nor is there any clear indication that he ever would have developed into a fine craftsman.

More significant is a wholly characteristic essay, "God's Lonely Man," which Wolfe rewrote at several stages of his career, and passages from which are scattered throughout *You Can't Go Home Again*. It is a final, comprehensive statement of a major theme of his life and work. He has lived, he says, "about as solitary a life as a modern man can have"; he has come to the complete conviction that loneliness is "the central and inevitable fact of human existence," and in this, not in conflict, is "the essence of human tragedy." Yet the lonely man, the tragic man who knows hideous doubt and despair, is also the joyful man, who loves life dearly and has the fullest sense of its wonder and glory. So it has been with all the great tragic writers, from Sophocles and Ecclesiastes to Dostoyevsky. The Old Testament in particular is "the most final and profound literature of human loneliness that the world has known." The way and meaning of Christ's life, Wolfe adds, is far better; Christ taught the life of love, and the faith in love triumphant. Nevertheless he cannot make this way his own, for all his experience has taught him that loneliness is "the everlasting weather of man's life," love only "the rare, the precious flower." This is indeed the consistent meaning of Wolfe's entire book. Among modern writers, only Conrad leaves so deep, persistent, haunting a sense of man's loneliness. In Conrad, however, there is less joy. Wolfe's conclusion is not mere resignation but a hymn of acceptance:

"Loneliness forever and the earth again! Dark brother and stern friend, immortal face of darkness and of night, with whom the half part of my life was spent, and with whom I shall abide now till my death forever—what is there for me to fear as long as you are with me? Heroic friend, blood-brother of my life, have we not coursed together the great and furious avenues of night, have we not crossed the stormy seas alone, and known strange lands, and come again to walk the continent of night and listen to the silence of the earth? Have we not been brave and glorious when we were together, friend? Have we not known triumph, joy, and glory on this earth—and will it not be again with me as it was then, if you come back to me? Come to me, brother, in the watches of the night. Come to me in the secret and most silent heart of darkness. Come to me as you always came, bringing to me again the old invincible strength, the deathless hope, the triumphant joy and confidence that will storm the earth again."

6. WOLFE AND THE TRADITION

"WHATEVER GEORGE WEBBER WAS," WOLFE WRITES IN *YOU CAN'T GO HOME AGAIN*, "he knew he was not an 'intellectual.' He was just an American who was looking hard at the life around him, and sorting carefully through all the life he had ever seen and known, and trying to extract some essential truth out of this welter of his whole experience." These are not humble words. Wolfe was proud to be not an intellectual, proud of all the truth he had extracted by himself, proud even of his apparent humility. Doubtless he was too proud, and therefore apt to magnify the difficulty of his achievement. More than once he explained his difficulties in these terms:

For he was united to no image save that image which he himself created. He was bolstered by no knowledge save that which he gathered for himself out of his own life. He saw life with no other vision save the vision of his own eyes and brain and senses. He was sustained and cheered and aided by no party, was given comfort by no creed, and had no faith in him except his own.

161

Of this, one may remark that Wolfe was aided by his editor, cheered by enthusiastic admirers, sustained by a great party of writers before him, comforted by a democratic creed; his faith was not so much a creation as a discovery of his heritage. Nevertheless these passages point to the essential quality of his achievement, and to his position in our letters. He was certainly not an intellectual, and stood outside the intellectual movements of his time; his career was a continuous self-education, an uncommonly stubborn, honest, arduous effort, religious in its intensity, to distill the truth and value of his experience; and even as a maverick he was an American through and through, exemplifying the most distinctive values and limitations of the native tradition.

Now, it should be clear that there is no necessary virtue in being non-intellectual. Wolfe could have been no less honest, thorough, and true to his experience had he been more intellectual, and he could have found his truth at much less cost of anguished confusion, with much less demand upon the reader's patience. Indeed, he could have got more of his feeling into his whole book. Feeling has to be penetrated and commanded by intellect before its full significance and force can be realized. The force of Wolfe's feeling is often dissipated by explosiveness in the early novels, and by a self-conscious, unaccustomed restraint in the later ones. Especially for the mythmaker in the modern world, flow or even form cannot take the place of intellect. The unfortunate American tendency to make a virtue of its absence, in the interest of "Life, Reality, and Experience," is exposed by the work of such Continental novelists as Silone, Malraux and Mann. They have been more di-

rectly and deeply involved in the immense, decisive conflicts of our time than have most American artists; but they
have also been better artists, treating these issues more im-
aginatively and more powerfully because they have an
intellectual command of the larger social, philosophical
implications, and a profound realization—in Silone's words
—that "they come from far and are going far."

Wolfe's limitations in this respect are emphasized when
George Webber begins to discover "whole series and sys-
tems of relations" between the thousands of things he had
observed. George, he writes, was "like a scientist in some
new field of chemistry who for the first time realizes that
he has stumbled upon a vast new world, and who will then
pick out identities, establish affiliations, define here and
there the outlines of sub-systems in crystalline union, without yet being aware what the structure of the whole is like,
or what the final end will be." The comparison calls attention not only to the rudimentariness of Wolfe's belated discoveries but to fundamental relations he ignored. For this
is one of his very rare references to science. He seems un-
concerned about, almost unaware of the force that is
largely responsible for the vast new world he was trying to
understand. He never discusses it, almost never alludes to
it or draws upon it for his metaphors; except for a few
Freudian terms, it is not in the background of his thought
or the texture of his language. And though the novelist is of
course not required to be a sociologist, or to discuss explicitly the deep causes of social change, Wolfe repeatedly
does discuss relatively superficial issues, the intellectual
fashions of the period. He also calls attention to his limitations by an indiscriminate attack on intellectuals, in which

163

he annihilates not only the "devoto-bloato wire-pullers and back-scratchers" but all the "franky-panky, seldesey-weldesey, cowley-wowley, tatesy-watesy, hicksy-picksy, wilsony-pilsony, jolasy-wolasy, steiny-weiny, goldly-woldly, sneer-puss fellows." Some of these writers have survived this annihilation.

Yet it should also be clear that an intellectual Wolfe would have been an entirely different writer, and not necessarily a better one. In art, qualities cannot be added without modifying other qualities; one plus one may make three, or may make nothing. An intellectual Wolfe would hardly have written *Look Homeward, Angel*, which is worth having as it is. The actual Wolfe was an "innocent man" discovering life. His innocence is the source of the extravagance and confusion of his legend, the occasional falsity; it is also the source of its freshness and immediacy, the distinctive kind of truth. As he grew wiser, he lost some of his strength.

Among many other things, Wolfe has been called an "elephantine Proust"; but the comparison emphasizes chiefly the essentially different quality of his mind and art. Both writers sought to recapture their whole past experience, by wringing the full significance from their sensory impressions. Both believed that this "subjective" enterprise was the best means to universality. Wolfe, however, had nothing like Proust's "thinking mastery of the unthinkable," the extraordinarily acute powers of analysis that enabled Proust to track down every fugitive sensation, to define it with unerring precision, to exhaust its whole intellectual and emotional content, and thus to assimilate and dominate his entire experience. Wolfe stayed much closer to the immediate impression or to the immediate emotion it induced; he rendered a great deal more than he explained, or could explain; and when he began to dwell on relations, they were generally broad relations that required no keen intelligence to perceive. But for the same reason he was less intensely subjective. He had a firmer grasp of the basic uniformities of human experience, the immediate appearances that are also "real," the elemental emotions that are also ultimate—the solid substance of life that Proust refined away to the point where, as William Empson has said, his work often reads like a superb appreciative criticism of a novel that has unfortunately not survived. Above all, Wolfe proved his thought and feeling by active experience, constant adventure; whereas Proust's interminable reflections were an essentially passive interpretation of a life already spent, or misspent.

Altogether, Wolfe's simplicity was not simple stupidity, or incapacity for thought. He indeed looked very hard at the life around him, he sorted through a vast deal of experience, and he constantly learned from experience. If he had more to learn than did any other contemporary writer of importance, if his readers (not to mention his mother) often have to pay the bills of his prolonged education, he is nevertheless distinguished by the thoroughness of this education. Because he had to learn the most elementary lessons, he really learned the living truth in platitudes that less innocent writers take for granted, and as easily forget. He acquired a full, intimate knowledge of the main highways of the general life, the main terms of man's hope and man's fate. He knew more possibilities of joy and of sorrow than intellectuals are apt to, and was less inclined to deny real goods or discount real evils. The great advantage of his way was that it enabled him, within the limits of his intellectual reach, to live and write as a whole man.

2

As a whole man, Wolfe was not "just an American"; or we might say that he approached the best in Americanism, which is cosmopolitanism, the ideal of a universal humanity. But he was first and last an American, and as such must be considered in the first and last analysis. A convenient approach to his position in our letters, accordingly, is through Alexis de Tocqueville's *Democracy in America.* Although written more than a hundred years ago, it remains perhaps the shrewdest, most objective analysis of the native tradition, in particular of the old America in which Wolfe had his roots.

The practical-minded American, Tocqueville remarked, is not really inspired by ideas of the supernatural, of Nature, of anything external to man. On the other hand, his daily concerns are not dignified by the manners, rituals, or pieties of an ancient culture: "Nothing conceivable is so petty, so insipid, so crowded with paltry interests—in one word, so anti-poetic—as the life of a man in the United States." But the American is inspired by the image of the whole nation—marching across the wilds, "turning the course of rivers, peopling solitudes, and subduing nature." Such an image of the vast democracy naturally leads to an idea of a still vaster drama, the vicissitudes of the whole human race. And with this exalted idea the individual can return to himself and gaze at a soul no longer puny: "I need not traverse earth and sky to discover a wondrous object woven of contrasts, of infinite greatness and littleness, of intense gloom and amazing brightness, capable at once of exciting pity, admiration, terror, contempt. I have only to look at myself." In short, the writer in a democracy cannot use the traditional themes of great poetry; the resources of ancient, aristocratic cultures fail him; but Man remains. "The destinies of mankind, man himself . . . with his passions, his doubts, his rare prosperities and inconceivable wretchedness, will become the chief, if not the sole, theme of poetry among these nations."

The poetic, not the realistic sense of life has indeed dominated our literature, at least until this century; and the sources of poetry defined by Tocqueville were the sources of the American Renaissance. These were the deepest sources of Wolfe's inspiration. He looked at himself and saw Jason, Dedalus, Telemachus, Faustus, Proteus, Antaeus, Prometheus—he saw Man, in his infinite possibilities. He looked around him and saw America, a new and potentially glorious chapter in the history of Man. Man stood in the presence of Nature, possibly of God, but he stood erect in the foreground, and their presence had meaning only because of his presence. Even in his apparent passion for nature, Wolfe was celebrating chiefly the immensity and grandeur of the American continent; he dwelt on the wild, savage, desolate aspects of nature that were an appropriate background for his own stormy passions as God's lonely American; and the majestic hills, which stirred his imagination chiefly as the "hills beyond," were perhaps less haunting than the whistle-wail of a man-made train snaking through the valleys at night.

167

To be sure, Man has always been the study of mankind. Yet this has not always been considered a proper study, or a sufficient one. It has evident limitations and dangers. In Tocqueville's view, these sources of poetry in a democracy are grand, but they are not abundant. "They are soon exhausted; and poets, not finding the elements of the ideal in what is real and true, abandon them entirely and create monsters." Hence he did not believe that literature in a democracy would prove insipid or earthbound; he believed rather that it would often be "surcharged with immense and incoherent imagery, with exaggerated descriptions and strange creations," and would "lose itself in the clouds." Actually, American literature has tended to both extremes. Tocqueville might have anticipated that writers would come to dwell on daily life in a democracy, whether in patriotic pride or in revulsion. But elsewhere he points to a common source of both the earthbound realism and the cloudy romanticism in our literature:

In democratic communities, each citizen is habitually engaged in the contemplation of a very puny object: namely, himself. If he ever raises his looks higher, he perceives only the immense form of society at large or the still more imposing aspect of mankind. His ideas are all either extremely minute and clear or extremely general and vague; what lies between is a void.

It was this void that Wolfe sought to bridge. He was not entirely successful—he might have done better, again, had he been more intellectual. He was more successful, however, than most typically American writers, from Whitman to Sherwood Anderson. And though comparison in these terms will hardly determine his stature as an artist, it does

168

help to measure his accomplishment in the task he set himself as an American mythmaker.

The inevitable comparison is with Whitman (even though Wolfe declared he did not read him until critics pointed to their kinship). Among the first to speak of the "democratic faith," Whitman was a more spontaneous, whole-hearted poet of American democracy than Wolfe was. Despite his often strident individualism, he had a warmer love of common men (however "abnormal" this love) and a heartier comradeliness. Likewise he was much less troubled by the disparity between the soaring poetry of the American dream and the paltry, "anti-poetic" realities of everyday American life—a disparity which obsessed Wolfe to the end, and which he was never quite able to accept. Indeed, Whitman seldom saw any real disparity. For precisely this reason, however, a great deal of his later poetry is unsatisfying. He fulfilled Tocqueville's prophecy by losing himself in the clouds. Although he became more aware of the corruption, inequality and injustice of expanding America, he slighted these ugly realities in his poetry. He could not clearly account for them or place them—they were like the arbitrary villain in melodrama, whose role had dramatic value but no logical necessity. For he had become an habitual yea-sayer, impatient of fault-finding, who wanted to keep his affirmations sweeping and pure. He also kept them ambiguous, chanting now as a lusty naturalist and now as a mystical idealist, now as a homespun radical and now as an apostle of capitalism; but his ambiguities were due to vagueness and simple inconsistency, not to a conscious irony or an awareness of complexity.[1] He glorified his contradictions, singing "I am large, I contain multitudes"; but what he contained was all the contradictions of nineteenth-century America. So there remained a resounding void between his concrete perceptions and his extremely general ideas.

Wolfe did not bridge the void by any systematic philosophy of history, such as the Hegelian or the Marxist; his declared faith is not a reasoned argument and lacks a firm logical basis. Yet his vision was far more complex and realistic than Whitman's. He saw clearly not only the paltry interests that engross the agents of the American dream but the underlying evils that are part of the American way. He also saw connections, had some notion of the causes and consequences of these evils, and knew that they were not accidental or incidental. Above all, he comprehended them in a tragic view of human destiny. As Yeats remarked, Emerson and Whitman have come to seem superficial because they lacked the Vision of Evil. Emerson believed that evil is "merely private" and temporary, and asserted that "the first lesson of history is the good of evil." Whitman could even deny the reality of evil: "I am myself just as much evil as good, and my nation is—and I say there is in fact no evil." Wolfe believed that specific evils were remediable, or at least that we must live in this hope; but his belief and his hope were toughened by his knowledge that Evil is as old as Time.

[1] In his book on Whitman written during the heyday of Marxist criticism, Newton Arvin attempted to show that the final tendency of his work was in the direction of socialistic democracy. Arvin acknowledges, however, that only by treating Whitman with "the most elastic dialectical fullness" can one keep him on the side of the angels and make his myth stand up.

Similarly he had a keener, stronger sense of concrete reality than Emerson. Like Wolfe, Emerson stressed Flow, constantly introduced images of flowing. Unlike Wolfe, he believed that he could step out of time and the river into eternity. It was an exalted conviction, which enabled him to touch sublimity in his lofty moments; but it also enabled him to lose himself in the blue. Although he believed that the fact, as a symbol of the idea, had a "mythologic" significance, he was not really interested in facts. He was the less inclined to look at them because he found literally everything in himself. "In all my lectures," he said, "I have taught one doctrine, namely, the infinitude of the private man." Hence he also taught that "there is properly no history, only biography"; and logically he might have added, as Thoreau did, that there is only autobiography.

Nevertheless the private man does have finite relations, he has to live in history, he has to get along with a multitude of other private men, in a public world. Emerson remained too aloof from the actual conflicts in a democracy, as in any society, and in particular from the masses of common men. As F. O. Matthiessen has observed, his problem in philosophy was how to reconcile the individual with society, just as his problem in prose was how to connect his sentences into a paragraph. His theory of the self-sufficient individual involved him in the American tendency to standardization—infinite men, like aspirants to rugged individualism, come to look and think pretty much alike. Wolfe saw more real good and more real evil in men because he did not find so much divinity in Man, or such relatively easy access to eternity. He regarded his autobiography modestly, as a means to truth-seeking, not the

171

epitome of Truth, and the truth he learned is that the private man is a lonely man, finite, mortal and self-sufficient only as he realizes his dependence upon his fellows and accepts their common destiny.

Such partial comparisons are unfair, of course, to Whitman and Emerson. Their optimism was a natural reflection of their America, a youthful, confident, rapidly growing nation, whose noisy self-assertion could be pardoned as the exuberant expression of a sturdy self-reliance. Wolfe lived in a far more critical, skeptical age, and his America was reconsidering its dream in the light of a world depression, the aftermath of a world war. But the point of this comparison is not that Wolfe was a greater thinker or artist than they. It is simply that the native tradition needs to be disciplined, the national myth needs to be complicated and qualified, and that Wolfe did work to this end. For the greater American writers of the past have seldom managed to embrace and accept the incongruous realities of the national life. On the one hand, Hawthorne, Poe, Thoreau, Melville, Emily Dickinson, Henry James and Henry Adams were isolated from their society, aloof when not estranged. On the other hand, Whitman, Emerson, Alcott, Whittier, Longfellow and the other kindly graybeards intensified the incongruities by promoting the national idealism in an innocent or complacent disregard of the materialism of their society. And those, like Mark Twain, who really knew the country and the people seldom spoke out in entire frankness or with consistent clarity.

It hardly need be added that Wolfe does not always appear to advantage when set beside his spiritual forebears. It is worth comparing him with Herman Melville, however, for perhaps his closest affinities were with the author of *Moby Dick*. Melville too was a poet of democracy, resolved to write a great book on a great subject, who found the elemental, timeless patterns of the myth in the life of American whalers. He too was an Ishmael, a homeless spirit seeking a father. He too believed that *Ecclesiastes* was "the truest of all books," and had a vision of evil more complex and more intense than Wolfe's. He knew not only the "anti-poetic" realities but the falsities of American life; an ardent defender of democracy, he could still behold democracy as a "harlot on horseback . . . arch strumpet of an impious age." He knew the terrible possibilities of the gospel of individualism; among other things, *Moby Dick* may be regarded as the tragedy of unbridled individualism, because of which Captain Ahab lives and dies in an appalling loneliness, cut off from his fellows, yet involving them in his disaster. Above all, Melville knew the deep ambiguities and dubieties that underlie the natural and spiritual life of "ungodly, godlike" man. From this vision he suffered a more profound and far more protracted torment than did Wolfe, partly because he had to wrestle with the problem of evil on theological grounds, try to answer the unanswerable question of why God should choose to create so imperfect a world. His torment became too much for him; his masterpiece was followed by the nightmare of *Pierre*, and then by silence.[2] Only

[2] Some passages in *Pierre* suggest Wolfe at his Gantiest: "The cheeks of his soul collapsed in him; he dashed himself in blind fury and swift madness against the wall, and fell dabbling in the vomit of his loathed identity."

toward the end of a long, lonely life did he make his peace, which was the peace of resignation, with little faith or hope. In *Moby Dick*, however, he displayed an intellectual and artistic mastery of his materials such as Wolfe scarcely approached.

In deliberately magnifying the simple life of whalers, Melville succeeded in achieving genuine grandeur because, despite all his personal commentary, he had the impersonality of the old epic poets and mythmakers. Although he is as prolix as Wolfe, he is always detached; his fable remains clear and strong, his mighty symbolism is firmly controlled. But his peculiar genius is revealed in the rich texture of his epic, the subtle and elaborate ambiguities woven into an elemental fable. In addition to such obvious symbols as the immense Pacific, comparable to the lonely continent that is the background of Wolfe's legend, Melville introduces such metaphysical symbolism as the whiteness of the whale, capitalizing on all the associations of white with gladness, innocence, radiance, holiness—and also with nothingness, with grief, terror and awe. Similarly Melville's imagery has more intellectual content than Wolfe's. Wolfe rendered the sensory image for its own sake or for the sake of its immediate emotional associations; his reflective passages are usually detachable and often prosaic. Melville fused the sensory image and the philosophical reflection, because he was no less the poet when reflecting. ("How many, think ye," he remarks when Tashtego falls into the whale's head, "have likewise fallen into Plato's honey head, and sweetly perished there?") Although his prose-poetry can be tortured and far-fetched, as Wolfe's can be too loose or mechanical, at his best Melville achieves a fuller communication, in which his sensing, his feeling and his thought are one.

As we approach contemporary American literature, with the increasing refinement and diversification of the native tradition, the limitations of Wolfe's craftsmanship become more conspicuous. In the company of Henry James he may look ludicrous indeed—the yokel artist, all thumbs and elbows and rolling eyes. He looks awkward enough in the company of Willa Cather, Hemingway, Steinbeck, or many lesser writers. Yet no less conspicuous are the qualities that have led foreign critics to hail him as "a young Titan out of the New World," magnificently representative of "the authentic American genius." Granted that responsible American writers are not obliged to strain for the All-American novel, and that American genius is not the ultimate in genius, still there is rich soil in the New World. Wolfe towers above most of his contemporaries because he was so deeply rooted in his native soil and native tradition.

Accordingly Henry James suffers too when Wolfe is set beside him. With all his fine perception and exquisite craft, James was confined to a sharply circumscribed world, a world free from economic necessities and other elemental compulsions, a world of nice moral issues divorced as well from the basic intellectual and spiritual issues of modern life. Despite his distaste for the crudities of American life, he was remarkably insensitive to its root evils, so that he could write of the fine consciences of wealthy Americans abroad with scarcely a hint of the ruthlessness, corruption and blind greed that produced such wealth. In his own kind of innocence, he accepted without qualification

Hawthorne's idea of how hard it was to write a romance "about a country where there is no shadow, no antiquity, no mystery, no picturesque and gloomy wrong, nor anything but a commonplace prosperity, in broad and simple daylight, as is happily the case with my dear native land." Wolfe was never so innocent as this.

In a broader view, James is the extreme example of the genteel tradition which, since the Renaissance, has tended to transform literature into *belles lettres*, a luxury for the elite; which until recently blinded Americans to the fact that they had a culture of their own, because home-grown products were seldom refined; and which still shapes the common notion of culture as an elegant accomplishment— "classy" in every sense of the word. (In deploring the excesses of practical education in America, one may forget the thousands of schoolmarms who teach youngsters to write polite essays "On" some gentlemanly or ladylike topic.) Wolfe's youthful image of the Artist was also shaped by this genteel tradition. But essentially he belongs to a much older tradition—the genuinely classic tradition, from Homer to Shakespeare—in which literature drew freely upon folklore and all the resources of the commonwealth. He really possessed the folk possessions—of language, legend, song, humor, handicraft, feeling for family and for the land—that it is now fashionable to exploit, like antiques.

Wolfe's advantage in this possession is emphasized by the Southern renascence from which he kept aloof—the constellation that includes such distinguished writers as Ellen Glasgow, Allen Tate, Katherine Anne Porter, Elizabeth Madox Roberts, William Faulkner, John Crowe

Ransom, John Peale Bishop, Robert Penn Warren, Caroline Gordon, Cleanth Brooks and Eudora Welty. Although they manifestly do not constitute a homogeneous movement or school, they have generally been selfconscious Southerners, devoted to Southern culture. As critics, they have inclined to disparage Wolfe, dismissing him as a gifted barbarian when not attacking him as a renegade. They have also tended to be repelled by contemporary American life, excessively concerned about the purity and autonomy of literature, and of late excessively alarmed by the crudities of "literary nationalism." And their distress is not due simply to their aversion to a triumphant industrialism. The trouble is that they are not firmly rooted, not really at home in the South. Their characteristically fine, subtle artistry is characteristically modern but not a natural outgrowth of Southern tradition or natural expression of Southern culture today. Their abortive "agrarianism" was an effort to invent an appropriate culture, and a tacit confession that they were not richly nourished by any living tradition; from the actual agrarian life of the South —the life in particular of negroes and poor white sharecroppers—they are generally aloof. In short, they are perhaps more profoundly alienated from the South than was Wolfe, who fled it. He never lost his deep attachment to Old Catawba.

Allen Tate has noted parenthetically that the most widely popular of these writers was Elizabeth Madox Roberts. He did not note that she drew most fully and unselfconsciously upon rich folk materials, and like Wolfe was close to the elemental simplicities. But Tate's own defense of regionalism is the best lead to the source of

Wolfe's strength. Regionalism, he says, is a sense of local continuity in tradition and belief, and is therefore limited in space but not in time. It is opposed to the "provincialism" of the modern man, which is limited in time rather than space: the contemporary may be a man of the world, but he is typically cut off from the past, locked in the present. This is a valid and useful distinction, pointing to the abiding value of regionalism and to the real limitation of contemporary sophistication. It also suggests, however, the higher value of synthesis and transcendence. And, by Tate's criterion, Wolfe was something more than a regionalist, but nothing of the provincial: a regionalist who was not limited to his region, a modern man who was not limited to the contemporary world.

Thus Wolfe had a deep sense of the past—of his family, of Old Catawba, but also of America, of all mankind. He could take America for his subject as naturally as other writers took their local region; he was a national, not a nationalist. He could draw as naturally on older, wider traditions, and not merely because of his travels abroad; he knew instinctively that the world of tragedy, as Malraux has said, is always the ancient world. Yet Wolfe was not bound by the past. His work is more genuinely traditional because he did not worship Tradition; for the only use of tradition is to define and enrich the present, equip us for life here and now. Wolfe had a full, vivid sense of the present too, in its multiplicity, its uniqueness, and its insistent claims upon our attention and our attachment. Altogether, this is a rare combination in contemporary American letters. It explains the unusual richness, depth and power of Wolfe's realism.

178

By contrast, the innumerable studies of rural or regional life in America, whether fond or grim, have typically been confined to the region, remote from the main issues of the contemporary world. The best of them—the novels of Willa Cather, for example—have been retrospective, nostalgic, elegiac: memorials to a vanishing or vanished life. The innumerable studies of urban, industrial life, on the other hand, have typically been confined to the contemporary scene. Many, such as the novels of John Dos Passos and James Farrell, display great energy but a relative poverty of feeling, owing to a want of natural piety or feeling for continuity. Others have warmth or zest but suffer from the want of an adequate myth. Thus Theodore Dreiser penetrated the shams and delusions of American life, by virtue of his dogged honesty and peasant sympathy; but once beneath the surface he was lost, at the mercy of more fundamental delusions. Lacking roots in a native tradition, or any cultural tradition, he succumbed to the dismal pseudo-scientific mythology of Zola's naturalism, interpreting life in terms of "chemic compulsions." And Sinclair Lewis, who is wholly American in his energy, shrewdness and gusto, is almost wholly contemporary. As his spirits have flagged, he has been left with the habit of satire but an increasing uncertainty about just what he is satirizing and why.

Most instructive is the contrast provided by John Dos Passos. Geographically and sociologically, his *U.S.A.* is a still more extensive, detailed record of American life than Wolfe's; yet it is less convincing both as fiction and as document. Doubtless his chief limitation is a lack of Wolfe's elemental creative gift—Dos Passos is simply unable to create characters in whose destiny one can become intensely interested. In particular, however, his record is distorted and relatively shallow because behind it is no rich sense of tradition, regional or national. Despite all the Newsreels, Camera Eyes, biographies and other devices by which he sought to widen its implications, it is by Tate's definition a provincial work. In his subsequent disillusionment with orthodox Marxism, Dos Passos has also discovered the national myth. He has therefore celebrated it more fervently than Wolfe: "We must never forget that we are heirs to one of the grandest and most nearly realized world pictures in all history." But little or nothing of this picture is in *U.S.A.* Like F. Scott Fitzgerald, he at that time saw America dedicated only to "the service of a vast, vulgar, and meretricious beauty." Wolfe saw all this and much more.

3

Here, in contemporary America, is our first and last concern; for the immediate world is the only world we have. And here is the final significance of Wolfe for contemporaries: he made himself at home in this world. It was the sensible thing to do, but it is evidently not an easy thing for an American artist.

Early in the century, a common theme in American fiction was the escape—or tragic failure to escape—to the City, the symbol of freedom, culture and the full life. Then came a revulsion, and a common theme was the return to the farm or the hometown, symbols of the wholesome life. Today we hear that there is no place to go. W. P. Southard has recently written on behalf of the young writers who "are trying to discover where in this country of degenerate children an adult can live." In cities he can see only a "blatting arrogant debilitated vulgarity" or an "astonishing confident obscenity"; he would like to find a small, disciplined community that wants to stay small—but he knows "that our community will not support us." Delmore Schwartz, writing from an academic community, is more emphatic: there is no room in our materialistic society for "such a monster as the cultivated man." Even so sober a critic as Isaac Rosenfeld seems to take as a matter of course the impossible position of American artists, remarking offhand that "the serious American writer cannot but be alienated from American society, close though he may be to it, and much though he may wish to belong." Marjorie Brace adds the logical conclusion: the writer "cannot write seriously without alienating himself from the values of his society, and at the same time he cannot function apart from his audience."

Now, I do not believe that our writers are necessarily or actually in such a bad way. Many serious, cultivated men seem to be functioning well enough, possibly because they have some historical perspective. When our traditionalists and classicists look to the past, they see the great writers who embody their pure ideal, but they seldom see the very impure societies in which these writers lived, or the fate of these societies. They forget that many great writers in the past were also more or less alienated from their society. Euripides, Dante, Racine, Swift, Rousseau, Blake, Byron, Flaubert, Arnold and Turgenev are a few examples offhand; and some of these—notably Dante—have come to be regarded as the very symbol of their age. Artists as naturally tend to oppose as to accept the current imperatives of behavior and belief. Nevertheless, few rebels in the past utterly rejected their society or regarded their cause as hopeless; most were pointing to the future because they had faith in the efficacy of their ideals and of their art. And it is such faith that many contemporaries lack. They are inclined to regard our whole civilization as simply an abomination, and to suspect that the future will be still worse.

They may be right. Possibly our world is unworthy of our attachment; possibly we are living in an impossible age. Yet neither piety nor realism will permit us to take this for granted. As Whitehead has said, the present is holy ground: it contains all that there is—the past is summed up in it, the future is implicit in it. And so to return to Wolfe. He went through all this, experiencing alienation as intensely and thoroughly as any American writer; but he finally came out of it.

Thus he began, like so many, by fleeing to the City. When he was disenchanted, however, he did not go home again; he could appreciate Old Catawba and still know that it was no real haven. He labored prodigiously to assimilate the present in all its multitudinous diversity—to get into, not away from it all. He struggled against the very strong temptation to believe that he was too fine, rare, exquisite a spirit for this world, and that all his difficulties arose from its coarse, vulgar apprehensions. His central theme of a pilgrimage, with all its related motifs, comes down to the central problem of the sensitive individual in an untraditional society: the search for unity beneath the increasing division of labor and belief, for a community of faith and purpose beneath the specialization of activity, the diversity of interest, and the protestant individualism of industrial, democratic America. At length Wolfe found himself, by finding such a community. He realized the inevitable dependence of any individual on the group; he approached the ideal relation of the artist to his society, as a spokesman of the common faiths and purposes. And if his best work stems from the period of his estrangement, if his search for a father and a home is more memorable than the announcement of his arrival, the terms of his final reconciliation and acceptance are implicit in all his work.

To begin with, they are concrete terms. They embrace the immediate realities of life in an industrial civilization, the immediate causes of the distress of other contemporaries. Wolfe was as sensitive as anyone to the by-products of our industrial triumphs, the dreary monotony, ugliness, vulgarity, brutality and misery. He never reconciled himself to these human costs—as who should? Yet he was also sensitive to the peculiar values of the machine age, the new forms of beauty and truth, the actual and potential contribution to the greatness of America. He was thrilled by the great bridges, buildings, trains and liners; he saw poetry as well as power, high aspiration as well as greed, in all such symbols of man's conquest of nature. From the beginning he knew that this was always the way with man's works: nothing so glorious that it is not touched with vanity, nothing so commonplace that it is not touched with dignity. He was better able to put up with the attendant evils of the modern way because he was close to the actual

183

THOMAS WOLFE

life of the soil and therefore could not, like the Southern
agrarians, so easily recommend agriculture as "the best
and most sensitive of vocations," "a form of labor that is
pursued with intelligence and leisure." Moreover, he always took for granted what most of the agrarians have
since come to realize, sadly—that industrialism is an irre-
versible process, and there is no going back. If our civilization is destroyed and men start all over again, they may
stick to a simpler kind of society. Meanwhile we have to
make the best of this kind.

Likewise Wolfe accepted the conditions of a democratic
society. In a full awareness of the limitations of common
men, he still recognized a community of simple values, as
well as a common destiny that ultimately makes all men indeed equal. But here he was inevitably involved in philosophical issues. Like most Americans, and especially
those who distrust theory or philosophy, he had an excess
of philosophy, mostly unconscious; for his testament rests,
as the justification of the American tradition must finally
rest, on some metaphysical assumptions about the nature
of man and the universe. The issue here is forced by W. H.
Auden. Wolfe's fiction strikes him as "grandiose rubbish,"
and he attributes it to a "false conception of human
nature." After experimenting with various modern faiths,
Auden has returned to the doctrine of Original Sin; he declares that a democratic society must be grounded on the
presupposition that "men are equal not in their capacities
and virtues but in their natural bias toward evil." He
speaks here for a large and growing company. British
writers in particular—for example, Aldous Huxley, Evelyn
Waugh and Christopher Isherwood—have been heading

184

for Rome or India; even the worldly Maugham has toyed with mysticism; and we may expect to hear much more about the essential evil of man, or the essential vanity of all worldly interests, as men feel unable in any other terms to understand or cope with the monstrous folly and evil of our world.

Now I believe that Wolfe's mature conception of human nature was not false. Certainly he was not blind to the ancient evil—his deep consciousness of it was one reason why he was never taken in by the fashionable faiths that seduced Auden. He nevertheless felt, like most of the tragic poets before him, that man's fate is tragic because human sorrows are not the consequence merely of human evil, and because the frailty of man is also the source of his dignity and worth. In this view, the doctrine of original sin is as false to the actual complexities and paradoxes of the good life as is the opposite doctrine of natural goodness. But at least it should be clear that Auden is denying the historic faith of democracy. His premise that man is naturally evil is the premise of political thinkers like Machiavelli and Hobbes, and it is the logical basis of the absolutist, authoritarian state; children of original sin cannot be trusted with freedom. The democratic faith must rest on the assumption that in the mass, in the long run, men are fit to govern themselves, and have enough intelligence and virtue to be deserving of life, liberty and the pursuit of happiness. This faith is accordingly liable to arrogance and shallow optimism, as the history of America makes plain enough. But Wolfe is not guilty of these excesses.

Similarly with another fundamental (if generally unconscious) premise of historic democracy—the assumption that the active type of man who struggles against evils is more admirable than the passive type who endures them. Activism has been the basic tradition of the Western world since the Middle Ages; it is at the root of science, industrialism and democracy alike; it has found its fullest expression in America. The ultimate in this way of life is the Faustian life of Wolfe. Even after he sobered down he clung to its ruling principle, for the wisdom he learned was not the wisdom of resignation. At the end he had the typically American belief that "something should be done" about the evil he saw—something drastic, even to the complete reconstruction of our society; though just what or how he did not pretend to know. Today, however, the very principle of activism is under attack. Like T. S. Eliot, writers are turning to the quietism of the Christian tradition, or like Aldous Huxley to Hindu philosophy. Their attitude may be described as a "failure of nerve," a flight from reality. It may also be described as a rediscovery of the "perennial philosophy," the wisdom of the East. This way of life has an evident value, it worked for thousands of years in Egypt and India, it is recommended in the commonplaces even of Western moralists; and I can see no grounds for absolutely proving its inferiority to the American way. Nevertheless it is more compatible with a caste system than with a democracy. Democracy has logically encouraged a full, free development of human potentialities, and an effort to control circumstances rather than submit to them.

All this is to say that the democratic faith remains a faith, not a self-evident, universal truth. As a faith and a

186

hope Wolfe announced it. But this raises the final question about the adequacy and validity of his American myth. More important than the discovery of America, it has been said, was the invention of America. God was once the guarantor, if not the author, of American democracy. The universal moral law to which the founding fathers appealed was the law of God; the "natural rights" of man that supposedly antedated the state were God-given rights; and throughout their history Americans have taken for granted that their manifest destiny was underwritten by the constitution of the universe. (Even their very worldly activities were undertaken in the name of God, for "God helps those that help themselves"—and was notably beneficent to the pious industrialists and speculators of the last century, who helped themselves to a large share of the country's wealth.) Wolfe's catholicity stops short of God. In his lyrical epilogue he does hear a voice speaking of "a land more kind than home, more large than earth," but throughout his pilgrimage he never listened for such intimations of immortality. His actual theme was the transient life of man on this earth—"loneliness forever and the earth again!" His living faith was that man, with the courage of truth, could make a better life. Wolfe was religious only in the intensity with which he sought the truth.

Here again he is restating the traditional democratic faith in contemporary terms, naturalistic and humanistic. Possibly they are not the best terms; this faith has unquestionably been shaken by the decay of Christian faith. Nevertheless we cannot recover the traditional certitudes by a mere effort of will. The fact is that the only religion

possible for many men of good will is a religion of humanity, a natural idealism. And at least a robust faith is possible
on these terms. Wolfe is in line with such thoroughly characteristic Americans as William James and Oliver Wendell
Holmes, Jr. Far from being dismayed by their acknowledgment of ultimate uncertainty, they were the more devoted
to the democratic ideal; for they regarded the good life as
an adventure in an evolving, unfinished world, an experiment that is more hopeful as well as more dangerous because its conditions are not absolute and unalterable—an
experiment that both permits and demands freedom.
Whether or not it fails (as so many experiments in civilization have failed), we may say that American democracy,
in its ideal conception, and even in its limited realization,
is one of the great historic adventures of the human spirit.
And because the myth has traditionally been allied with
religion, we may add that the terms of Wolfe's myth not
only permit an epic grandeur but are not, at bottom, so
utterly different from the terms of the ancient epics.

Thus the Olympian gods of Homer have a clear dramatic
value, but little ideal or religious value. Their constant
meddling in human affairs is due to injured vanity or mere
caprice, not to any concern for justice. They have less dignity, in fact, than the human heroes, and are treated with
less respect by Homer. His men have their own values and
their own honor, and they go gallantly to their deaths in
the belief that their destiny is Hades—a darkness more
tangible than that which Wolfe saw enveloping the life of
man. Likewise the historic adventure of American democracy is at least as impressive and elevated as the Trojan
adventure that inspired Homer. In our realism and our

sophistication, we properly make reservations that Homer did not; we are perforce aware that the whole enterprise is also very gross and noisy, and that its most conspicuous motives are economic, not spiritual; and we are then likely to forget its heroic, epic quality. We are the more likely to disparage it because we seldom complicate the past as we do the present. In the fear that we may be living in the twilight of an age, we forget that Homer did live in such a twilight. He was celebrating a glorious past, not a glorious promise—his Achaean civilization was in fact entering the shadows.

We must then add, of course, that Wolfe was no Homer. The comparison emphasizes not only all the unheroic, inglorious qualities of his work but its incompleteness. At the end he had an exceptionally full sense of our whole situation, a clear image of our faith and our hope; he had not achieved a complete imaginative organization of our situation, an adequate symbolic expression of our faith and hope. The epical promise of America, in literature as in life, is still unfulfilled. "Probably we are still a folk," wrote Constance Rourke, "—an imperfectly formed folk— rather than a schooled and civilized people." Or perhaps we are an unhappy combination of folk and civilization; as a simple folk we might have had our Homer. Meanwhile we remain impatient for outcomes, as we have always been, and may grow weary of the everlasting promise that is always in the future. But meanwhile, too, I should say that Wolfe was our closest approach to a Homer. Given "the billion forms of America" and "the dense complexity of all its swarming life," his life work was perhaps as close as we can expect to come to an American epic.

BIBLIOGRAPHY

I. THOMAS WOLFE

A bibliography of Thomas Wolfe up to 1943 has been compiled by George R. Preston, Jr. and published by Charles S. Boesen, New York. It includes many short stories and sketches, but almost all of these later appeared either in the novels (in revised form) or in the volumes of collected pieces listed below.

Look Homeward, Angel. New York. 1929.

Of Time and the River. New York. 1935.

From Death to Morning. New York. 1935.

The Story of a Novel. New York. 1936.

The Web and the Rock. New York. 1939.

The Face of a Nation. Poetical passages from the writings of Thomas Wolfe, selected by John Hall Wheelock. New York. 1939.

You Can't Go Home Again. New York. 1940.

The Hills Beyond. New York. 1941.

Thomas Wolfe's Letters to His Mother. Edited with an introduction by John Skally Terry. New York. 1943.

A Stone, A Leaf, A Door. Poems by Thomas Wolfe selected and arranged in verse by John S. Barnes. New York. 1945.

BIBLIOGRAPHY

"A Western Journey." *Virginia Quarterly Review,* Summer, 1939. (Wolfe's last manuscript, with an introduction by E. C. Aswell.)

II. SECONDARY STUDIES

1. Books

Beach, Joseph Warren, *American Fiction: 1920–1940.* New York. 1941.

Cowley, Malcolm, *After the Genteel Tradition.* New York. 1937. (Contains an essay on Wolfe by Hamilton Basso.)

Geismar, Maxwell, *Writers in Crisis. The American Novel Between Two Wars.* Boston. 1942.

Kazin, Alfred, *On Native Grounds. An Interpretation of Modern American Prose Literature.* New York. 1942.

Muller, Herbert J., *Modern Fiction: A Study of Values.* New York. 1937.

2. Periodicals

Basso, Hamilton, "Thomas Wolfe: A Summing Up," *The New Republic,* September 23, 1940.

Bates, Ernest Sutherland, "Thomas Wolfe," *The English Journal,* September, 1937.

Bishop, John Peale, "The Sorrows of Thomas Wolfe," *The Kenyon Review,* Winter, 1939.

Burgum, Edwin Berry, "Wolfe's Discovery of America," *The Virginia Quarterly Review,* Summer, 1946.

DeVoto, Bernard, "Genius Is Not Enough," *The Saturday Review of Literature,* April 25, 1936.

Geismar, Maxwell, "Thomas Wolfe: The Hillman and the Furies," *The Yale Review,* Summer, 1946.

Macauley, Thurston, "Thomas Wolfe: A Writer's Problems," *The Publishers' Weekly,* December 24, 1938.

Powell, Desmond, "Wolfe's Farewells," *Accent,* Winter, 1941.

Schoenberner, Franz, "Wolfe's Genius Seen Afresh," *The New York Times Book Review,* August 4, 1946.

Simpson, Claude, "Thomas Wolfe: A Chapter in His Biography,"
The Southwest Review, April, 1940.

Volkening, Henry T., "Thomas Wolfe: Penance No More," *The
Virginia Quarterly Review*, Spring, 1939.

Warren, Robert Penn, "A Note on the Hamlet of Thomas Wolfe,"
The American Review, May, 1935.

INDEX

193

INDEX